# THEMES
## for early years

# PETS

LY ... SS

# THEMES
## *for early years*

**Author** Lynne Burgess
**Editors** Noel Pritchard and Joel Lane
**Assistant editor** Libby Weaver
**Series designer** Lynne Joesbury
**Designer** Toby Long
**Illustrations** Rachael O'Neill (Kathy Jakeman Illustration)
**Cover** Based on an illustration by Sue Coney
Action Rhymes, Poems and Stories compiled by Jackie Andrews
Songs compiled by Peter Morrell
Assemblies chapter by Lesley Prior
*For Andrew and Ryan*
Designed using Aldus Pagemaker
Processed by Scholastic Ltd, Leamington Spa
Printed in Great Britain by Hartnolls Ltd

Published by Scholastic Limited, Villiers House, Clarendon Avenue, Leamington Spa, Warwickshire CV32 5PR

© 1996 Scholastic Limited Text © 1996 Lynne Burgess

2 3 4 5 6 7 8 9     7 8 9 0

The publishers gratefully acknowledge permission to reproduce the following copyright material:
© 1995 **Clive Barnwell** for 'Pets'; © 1994 **Pat Thomson** for 'Drat that fat cat' from *A Band of Joining-in Stories* (Transworld); © 1992
**Sarah Matthews** and the author's estate for 'Barney and Fred' from *Animal Poems* by Stanley Cook, (Simon & Schuster); © 1995
**Jean Gilbert** for 'Pets need looking after'; © 1995 **Kate Harrison** for 'Jumping here, jumping there' from *Look! Look what I can do*
(BBC Books); © 1995 **Ian Henderson-Begg** for 'Granny Davey's house'; © 1990 **David Higham Associates** for 'Morag and the lamb'
by Joan Lingard (Walker Books); © 1995 **Jan Holdstock** for 'Come to the pet shop', 'The rabbit's warning', 'Naughty little kitten'
and 'I'm a dog with a job'; © 1995 **Barbara Ireson** for 'Robin Redbreast and Puss' from *Over and Over Again* (Beaver Books);
© 1995 **Jan Jones** for 'Cats'; © 1995 **Karen King** for 'Katy's pets'; © 1995 **Wes Magee** for 'Pet fingers', 'My dog's first poem' and
'But me?'; © 1995 **Tony Mitton** for 'Pet riddles' and 'Who took the cheese?'; © 1995 **Peter Morrell** for 'My dog Sandy'; © 1995
**Judith Nicholls** for 'Pet talk'; © 1995 **Gillian Parker** for 'Who am I?'; © 1995 **Jan Pollard** for 'Black cat' and 'Guinea-pigs';
**Murray Pollinger** for © 1991 Joyce Dunbar 'The way out' by Joyce Dunbar from *Bedtime Stories for the Very Young* (Kingfisher);
© 1995 **Lesley Prior** for Assemblies; © 1995 **John Rice** for 'Next door's dinosaur'.
Every effort has been made to trace copyright holders and the publishers apologise for any inadvertent omissions.

**British Library Cataloguing-in-Publication Data** A catalogue record for this book is available from the British Library.

ISBN 0-590-53383-5

The right of Lynne Burgess to be identified as the Author of this work has been asserted by her in accordance with the Copyright,
Designs and Patents Act 1988.

# CONTENTS

THEMES *for early years*

# INTRODUCTION

'Pets' is a favourite cross-curricular theme for early years pupils. It is an ideal way of introducing children to animals and their basic life processes. Most young children are fascinated by pets and are keen to find out more about them. Many will either have pets of their own or know friends, relatives or neighbours who have them.

Organising a topic can be a demanding and time-consuming task. This book aims to help early years educators by providing a comprehensive starting-point for the 'Pets' topic. It includes a detailed topic web to show the overall relationship of the topic to all areas of the curriculum; ideas for stimulus displays; assemblies and suggestions for activities. Photocopiable sheets at the end of the book link with specific activities and offer a useful method of recording. Finding relevant resources for a topic can often prove difficult, so a selection of stories, rhymes and songs is included together with a recommended resources list.

## USING THEMES

A topic on 'Pets' can be approached in a variety of ways through different sub-themes. Each of the first five activity chapters in this book focuses on a different type of pet. The types include dogs (Chapter 1), cats (Chapter 2), guinea-pigs (Chapter 3), fish (Chapter 4) and rabbits (Chapter 5). Chapter 6 features activities based on 'the pet shop'.

This topic will allow children to find out more about animals by comparing common features such as their physical characteristics, feeding habits, senses, behaviour, growth and movement. It will also provide an opportunity for children to experience a special friendship with an animal and develop a sense of responsibility for the care of living things.

Throughout the topic, it will be important for the children to have firsthand experience of pets. Although secondary sources such as books and photographs will enrich the topic, handling real animals is essential. Arrange for a pet owner to bring his pet into the nursery for an hour or two, or borrow a pet for a day or a week. Apart from using the children's own pets, try inviting a local vet, specialist animal breeders, rescue organisations or pet shop owners to visit the school.

Whenever an animal is brought in, it is essential to treat it humanely and to consider its needs. The children should be sitting quietly to receive their visitor and so avoid frightening the animal. They should be taught how to handle the pet correctly and to take turns to touch it. If a pet is to be kept on the premises for any period of time, make sure it is housed and fed properly. Always use fish tanks and not fish bowls. Guidelines on keeping pets are often produced by local education authorities, while other important sources of information are the DFE (*Animals and Plants in Schools: Legal Aspects*) and the RSPCA (*Animals in Schools*) booklets. See page 96 for contact addresses.

Similarly, it is vital to consider the children in your care. Be sensitive to children who may be frightened of animals, and find out whether any children suffer from allergies. Also bear in mind the possibility of cultural differences in attitudes towards pets. Always check that an animal is used to children and safe to touch, and never leave children unsupervised with a pet. Remember to emphasise the importance of hygiene, and make sure the children always wash their hands after handling pets.

## CROSS-CURRICULAR LINKS

Cross-curricular topics are popular with early years teachers because they mirror the way young children learn. Subject boundaries do not exist for this age group, in which children automatically make links across the curriculum. While a topic on 'Pets' will have a strong science focus, it will also develop skills in English (listening, talking, recording) and Mathematics (counting, shape, pattern, sizes). Many of the Arts areas (drama, dance, art and music) will also arise spontaneously as children move like pets, draw their observations and learn songs. A topic on 'Pets' will also encourage the children to respect animals and develop a responsible attitude towards caring for them.

# HOW TO USE THIS BOOK

The wealth of material in this book will help you to plan work for several weeks, if not a whole term. The length of time spent on the topic will depend greatly upon the response of the children. Very young children may only be able to sustain interest in, and enthusiasm for, a topic for a short period. However, by dividing the topic into shorter sub-themes, the children's natural curiosity can easily be rekindled as each new aspect of the topic is introduced.

## TEACHING STRATEGIES

The content of this book has deliberately been organised to allow flexibility of use. Some teachers will wish to use the majority of the material, while others may find it a useful dip-in resource to supplement their own ideas. In either case, it is important to adapt activities and choose resources to suit the needs of the individual children in your early years setting.

Similarly, there is no need to tackle the activities in exactly the same order as they are presented in the book. You may decide to begin your topic with a visit to a pet shop, in which case Chapter 6 may become your starting-point. The activities within each chapter can also be used in any order.

## TOPIC WEB PLANNING

The topic web on pages 8-9 aids planning by showing clearly how each activity relates to the National Curriculum and the Scottish 5–14 Guidelines. To make sure that the children receive a broad and balanced curriculum, the topic web has been designed with an even distribution of activities between subjects.

Although each activity has one main subject focus, most will also make important contributions to other subject areas. For example, an activity which has been identified as having a chiefly mathematical basis will often introduce new vocabulary and so develop children's language skills.

## ACTIVITY PAGES

Each chapter in this section focuses on a particular theme of the 'Pets' topic. A wide variety of activities are suggested, each one linked to a different subject in the curriculum. The main elements within each activity are listed below.

### Objective
This identifies the main subject area and explains the purpose of the activity. Many of the activities, however, will involve skills from more than one curriculum area.

### Group size
A suggestion is given for the appropriate group size, but individual circumstances may influence your choice of the number of children in the group. For example, the presence of adult helpers may mean that more children can undertake the activity than is suggested here.

### What you need
This provides a list of materials and equipment needed before the activity can begin.

### Preparation
Preparation work is necessary for some activities. This may involve making or setting out equipment. Alternatively, the children may need prior experience or knowledge which is essential to the success of the activity.

### What to do
Step-by-step instructions are outlined on how to introduce the activity, and guidance is offered on what the children should do. Although precise instructions are given, a certain amount of flexibility is needed, and most of the activities can be adapted for different ability levels.

### Discussion

This section outlines the main points to talk about with the children, though it is important to adopt a flexible approach and allow the children to lead the conversation into other, equally valid areas. Some activities may involve adult intervention throughout, while others may lend themselves to a summary discussion after the children have completed the task. Whenever possible, encourage the children to discuss ideas with a friend, an older child or an adult helper as well as yourself.

### Follow-up activities

This section contains ideas for extending each activity, both within the same subject area and into associated areas. Be prepared to follow up any idea suggested by the children, even if it moves the topic on to a slightly different area you had not originally intended to cover. It is important to allow the children some self-directed tasks.

## DISPLAYS

This chapter suggests ideas for setting up stimulus displays linked to the various themes in this book. For each display, there is a list of the materials required, instructions on how to assemble them and points for discussion. Most of the displays are interactive, to encourage the children to become actively involved. Whenever possible, encourage the children to help gather and select resources, and allow them to help assemble the display. Always allocate sufficient time for the children to examine the displays individually, and organise a group or class discussion time to talk about them.

## ASSEMBLIES

This chapter provides ideas for planning assemblies related to the theme of 'Pets'. Each assembly plan contains practical ideas on how the children can contribute, ways in which they can be encouraged to reflect on the theme they are covering, a suggested theme for prayer and a song.

## RESOURCES SECTION

These chapters contain a useful selection of stories, poems, action rhymes and songs which link specifically with the 'Pets' topic. Much of the material is new and has been specially commissioned to complement this topic. All of these resources are photocopiable.

## PHOTOCOPIABLE ACTIVITY SHEETS

This section includes eight pages of photocopiable activities. Each page links with a specific activity detailed earlier in the book. It is important to make sure that the children understand how to complete each sheet, and that any new vocabulary is explained. Allow time to discuss the completed sheet with each child in order to find out how much they have understood.

## RECOMMENDED MATERIALS

This section gives details of story-books, information books, poetry, songs and works of art linked to the 'Pets' topic. Many of these resources can be borrowed from local libraries. Also remember to ask the children to bring in their own favourite stories, poems and songs which focus on the topic.

## EXPRESSIVE ARTS

*Planning towards the National Curriculum and the Scottish National Guidelines 5-14*

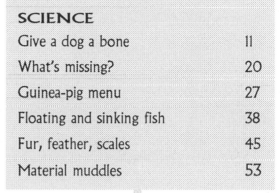

## ENVIRONMENTAL STUDIES

# PREPARING FOR PRIMARY SCHOOL

The children in any early years setting are individuals, and many will be at very different stages of development. Whatever level they have reached, it is important to help prepare a sound foundation from which children can go on to study the subjects of the National Curriculum. This can easily be achieved through many everyday play activities.

The National Curriculum was established to standardise the subjects, and subject content, taught at all levels of a child's education. It is intended that any child will be able to go to school anywhere in the country and find the same areas of the curriculum being covered. These subjects are: English Language, Mathematics, Science, History, Geography, Design and Technology, Information Technology, RE, Art, Music and PE.

Most of the activities suggested in this topic are based on common play activities such as dressing up, drawing, using construction toys or making puppets. However, each activity also has a specific objective: to develop important skills in preparation for the first stage of the National Curriculum.

## TOWARDS LEVEL ONE

National Curriculum learning requirements do not apply until children reach the age of five. The National Curriculum programmes of study were therefore written to suit the abilities of children who have reached their fifth birthday and who, depending on the part of the country in which they live, have spent from a term to a year in a Reception class. The National Curriculum provides an overall programme of study for each subject, and asks teachers to assess the level of attainment of every child when he or she reaches Year Two. This assessment is carried out partly through nationwide testing; but for the most part, it is left to the teacher's professional judgement to allocate an overall level to each child.

By the time children begin Level 1, they will need to have developed vital learning skills. These include communication, observation, social and physical skills. The activities suggested in this book allow these vital skills to be developed through firsthand experience.

The Topic Web on pages 8–9 also shows how the learning objective of each activity relates to the subject areas of the National Curriculum.

## THE SCOTTISH NATIONAL GUIDELINES 5–14

In Scotland, there are National Guidelines for schools on what should be taught to children between the ages of five and fourteen.

These National Guidelines are divided into six main curriculum areas: English Language, Mathematics, Environmental Studies, Expressive Arts, Religious and Moral Education, and lastly Personal and Social Development.

Within these main areas, further subjects are found – for example, 'Expressive Arts' includes art and design, drama, music and PE. Strands are also identified within each subject – for example, 'Mathematics' includes 'problem-solving and enquiry', and 'shape, position and movement'.

Most nurseries will find that the experiences they are offering children will provide a good foundation for this curriculum. The activities in this book have been specially written to prepare for many aspects of it, and will also fit well into the pre-five curriculum guidelines issued by local authorities throughout Scotland.

We have organised the activities into separate areas of the curriculum on the Topic Web (see pages 8–9) to help you with your planning. The children's personal and social development is an ongoing theme which is incorporated throughout the activities in this book.

# CHAPTER 1
# DOGS

Most young children are likely to be familiar with dogs as family pets. Extend their understanding by comparing and contrasting the size and appearance of different breeds of dog. As well as looking at pet dogs, find out about 'working' dogs such as police dogs, sheep dogs and dogs used by the blind, deaf or disabled.

## GIVE A DOG A BONE

### Objective

Science – To record information about the physical characteristics of dogs.

### Group size

Any size.

### What you need

A (real) dog, a display board, blue backing paper, white paper, a stapler, paints, scissors, felt-tipped pens.

### Preparation

Staple the backing paper on to the display board. Cut bone shapes from the white paper (each long enough to write a short phrase on).

### What to do

Show the real dog to the children and talk about the dog's physical characteristics.

After the group discussion, suggest that each child chooses a different attribute of the dog and writes it on one of the bone-shaped pieces of paper. An adult can act as scribe for younger children.

Choose one child to paint a large picture of the dog. When this is dry, cut it out and staple it in the middle of the display board. Add a label at the top asking 'What have we found out about Barney?' and then staple the bone shapes around the painting of the dog.

### Discussion

Name and talk about the body parts of the dog. What colour and type of coat does he have? How many legs? What shape are his ears? Does he make any noises?

Discuss the final display. Count the number of different bones on the board. Ask individuals to read out the information on the bone shapes. Encourage the children to continue to add more information in the following days.

### Follow-up activities

✧ Use pencils to draw pictures of the dog, showing as many body parts as possible.
✧ Compare and contrast photographs of a dog as a puppy and as an adult.
✧ Sing 'My Dog Sandy' (see page 83 of the Resources section).

# GOOD DOG

### Objective

English – To write a book of commands which dogs should obey.

### Group size

Any size.

### What you need

Coloured card, white paper, pencils, wax crayons, scissors, adhesive, a stapler, a camera.

### What to do

Invite the owner of a well-trained dog to visit and demonstrate how the dog responds to a variety of commands. The dog could be a pet or a 'working dog' such as a police dog, sheep dog or a dog for deaf, blind or disabled people. Take photographs of the dog and its handler.

Suggest that each child draws and colours a picture of herself giving a command to a dog. Write the command on each finished picture in a speech bubble coming from the mouth of the child.

Mount all the children's drawings on card and staple these into a book. Ask one or two children to design a cover for the book. Display the finished book alongside photographs of the dog and dog handler and pictures of other 'working dogs'.

### Discussion

Encourage the children to listen carefully for the words the handler uses to instruct the dog. Is the same word always used for one task – for example, to ask a dog to fetch? Is the command long or short? How does the handler use her voice or gestures to help the dog understand?

Invite the children to read the book they have made, individually or as a group. Ask a child to talk about either her own picture or someone else's. Can the rest of the group identify the command being given in the picture without reading the speech bubble?

### Follow-up activities

✧ Suggest that the children work in pairs and act out the roles of dog and handler. What does the handler train the dog to do, and how does the dog respond?

✧ Make up a story about a disobedient dog. Sit a group of children in a circle and ask them to take turns to add the next sentence to the story.

✧ Sing 'I'm a Dog with a Job' (see page 86 of the Resources section).

# ONE-TO-ONE CARDS

## Objective

Mathematics – To practise matching with one-to-one correspondence.

## Group size

Small groups of up to six children.

## What you need

Large sheets of coloured card, felt-tipped pens, scissors, adhesive plastic film, eight envelopes.

## Preparation

Cut out eight pieces of card (A4 size or larger). On each card, draw or stick a different number of pictures of dogs (between two and ten). These could be hand-drawn, made using a rubber stamp or cut from magazines. Cut out eight more pieces of card and on each one, draw and colour a set of objects associated with dogs (such as bones, collars, dishes, leads, balls, rings, tins of dog food and dog biscuits). Again, each set should show a different number of objects between the numbers two and ten. Cut out the individual sets of objects, then cover the sets of objects and the dog cards with adhesive plastic film. Stick an envelope on to the back of each dog card and place one set of objects in each envelope. The number of dogs on the dog card does not have to correspond to the number of objects in the envelope attached to that card. (See Figure 1.)

## What to do

Give each child a dog card and ask them to remove the pictures from the envelope on the back. Invite them to match the objects to the dogs by placing one picture beside each dog on the card.

Encourage the children to try this with as many dog cards as possible.

## Discussion

Emphasise the importance of only matching one object to one dog. Talk about the numbers of dogs (and objects) for a given dog card. Are there enough bones for each dog? Are there more leads or more dogs? Which cards have the same number of objects and dogs?

## Follow-up activities

✧ Use photocopiable sheet 88 to record one-to-one correspondence, emphasising that there is no one 'correct' answer.
✧ Ask a small number of children to pretend to be dogs. Choose individuals to mime giving one dog biscuit to each dog.

Figure 1

# MONOPRINT DOG

## Objective

Art – To introduce monoprinting and focus on the use of line.

## Group size

Small groups of up to six children.

## What you need

Access to a real dog, pictures of various breeds of dog, a polythene sheet, aprons, finger paints (white, brown and black), three spoons, two printing rollers for each child, implements for making a variety of lines (plastic modelling tools, lollipop sticks, matchsticks, toothbrushes, old pencils, old paintbrushes, straws, sticks and twigs, cotton buds, feathers), sugar paper (beige, dark brown and black).

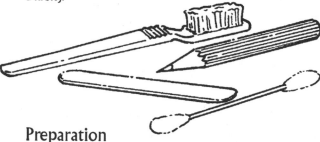

## Preparation

Invite a dog owner to bring his dog into the nursery and encourage the children to look at it closely. Focus on its colour, shape and size and name various body parts. Describe the texture of its fur. Is it the same all over?

Look at the pictures of dogs and compare and contrast these with the dog the children have met. Ask them to sort the pictures into two sets: the dogs with short fur and the dogs with long fur.

## What to do

Cover a table with a large sheet of polythene. Make sure the children are wearing aprons, preferably with sleeves.

Ask them to choose one of the finger paint colours with which to print their picture of a dog. Spoon out the chosen colour on to the polythene and spread the paint evenly using the printing roller.

Experiment with each tool to discover what kind of mark it will make. Use the printing roller to

spread the paint evenly again before asking the children to work individually to draw a dog in the paint using the various implements.

When the picture is finished, help the children to place the sugar paper over the picture and gently run a clean printing roller over the top of it. Peel the paper off the paint to reveal the print. Display the finished pictures.

## Discussion

Talk about what is happening to the roller and the paint. As the children experiment with the implements, observe the marks each one produces. Which ones make thick or thin lines? How can you make short spiky marks or long wavy lines? Do both ends of the implement produce the same mark? Relate these marks to the drawing of a dog.

When the children choose their sheet of sugar paper, discuss their choice of colour. Is it sensible to choose black paper if you are using black finger paint? Discuss the final print. Is the image clear, or are some areas difficult to distinguish? How could this problem be remedied?

## Follow-up activities

✧ Challenge the children to experiment further. How many prints can they take from their picture? Alter the picture or add another colour, and take new prints for comparison with the first set.
✧ Invite the children to choose a name for their dog. Write the name on a piece of paper in the shape of a dog bowl, colour or decorate it and staple it below the print.
✧ Read the poem 'My Dog's First Poem' on page 70 of the Resources section.

# BUILD A KENNEL

## Objective

Technology – To build a simple kennel for a soft toy dog.

## Group size

Small groups of up to six children.

## What you need

Three soft toy dogs, a picture of a kennel, construction toys (such as building bricks, Duplo or Bauplay).

## What to do

Talk about the picture of the kennel with the children, since not all of them will have seen one. Show them the three soft toy dogs and suggest that they work in pairs to build a kennel for one of the dogs. Allow the children to choose the type of construction material they will use.

## Discussion

Discuss the function of a kennel and the materials that have been used to build the one in the picture. As the children build their kennel, talk about the materials (plastic, wood) and shapes (cubes, cylinders) they are using. Will their kennel have a flat or a pointed roof? Is a window necessary? Encourage the children to check regularly to make sure the soft toy dog will fit into the kennel.

When all the kennels are finished, encourage the pairs in the group to assess each other's designs. Does each dog fit into its kennel comfortably? Are there any problems and how can these be solved?

## Follow-up activities

✧ Suggest that the children draw pictures of the finished kennels, showing the construction materials used.

✧ Compare and contrast the designs of two or three different types of dog bed.

# PASS THE BONE

## Objective

PE — To take part in a simple team game.

## Group size

Small groups of up to six children.

## What you need

Three soft toy dogs, three cardboard bone shapes with a string necklace attached (see Figure 1), access to a large open space, sand timers (five minute, three minute and one minute).

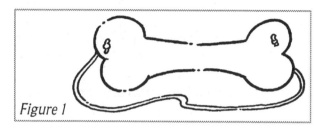
Figure 1

## What to do

Ask the children to sort themselves into pairs and show them where to stand (see Figure 2). Place the three soft toy dogs at the finishing line. Put the bone necklace around child A in each pair and explain that at a given signal (shout 'Woof!'), child A has to move on all fours like a dog and take the bone to child B. The bone necklace is then put on child B who moves on all fours, taking the bone to the soft toy dog. The winning team is the first to take their bone to the soft toy dog.

Alternatively, use a sand timer to limit the time available. Can the children take the bone to the soft toy dog before all the sand runs through? Start with a five-minute timer and then repeat the activity, reducing the time allowed.

## Discussion

Talk about any problems involved in moving on all fours or taking the bone necklace on and off. Warn the children to be careful when removing the necklace. Allow them to repeat the activity several times and discuss whether they feel their speed improves with practice. If using a sand timer, talk about how difficult it is to complete the game within the different time limits.

## Follow-up activities

✧ Make the game more demanding by suggesting that the children take several bones (one at a time) to the soft toy dog. How many can they take in a set time?
✧ Invite the children to make up their own dog and bone game.
✧ Show the children real bones and talk about why dogs like to chew on them. Compare a real bone with synthetic alternatives.
✧ Read the poem 'The Diners in the Kitchen' (see Recommended Materials list, page 96).

Figure 2

# WALKING THE DOG

### Objective

Geography — To introduce simple map-reading skills.

### Group size

Small groups (up to six children).

### What you need

Four easily-recognisable objects (bean bag, hoop, PE mat, rope), a photocopier, felt-tipped pens, clear plastic wallets, three soft toy dogs on leads (tie ribbon or string round each one).

### Preparation

Place four objects (bean bag, hoop, PE mat, rope) in different positions on the floor in a large space. Draw a simple map to show the position of each object and make four or five photocopies of this map. Colour the objects to make it easier to identify them and draw a different route on each map. (Use a cross to show where to start, a dotted line for the route and a spot to show where to stop — see Figure 1.) Place each map in a clear plastic wallet.

### What to do

Ask the children to identify each object on the floor and then point to the corresponding picture on the map. Suggest that they work in pairs to take one of the dogs for a walk. Give each pair a map to show the route of the walk. Allow the children enough time to walk their dog along their route and then ask each pair to demonstrate their walk to the rest of the group.

Invite the children to swap dogs and maps and repeat the activity.

### Discussion

If the children are experiencing any difficulties in following the map, talk with them to help solve the problem. As each pair demonstrate their walk, ask the others to check that they are following the route correctly. Encourage the children to use precise positional language when discussing the route or the maps (for example, *inside* the hoop, *on* the mat, *beside* the bean bag, *in between* the rope and the mat).

### Follow-up activities

✧ Give the children photocopies of the map and ask them to draw on their own routes for other children to follow.

✧ Repeat the activity using maps of a more complex area, such as part of the classroom or an outdoor play area.

✧ Read the story 'Morag and the Lamb' on page 78 of the Resources section.

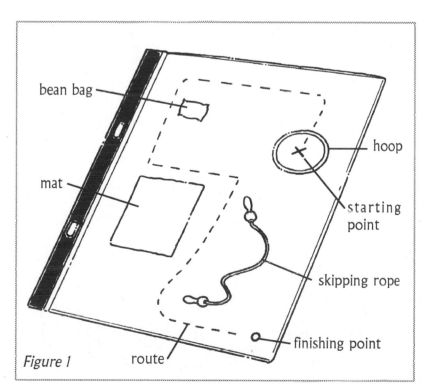

bean bag
mat
hoop
starting point
skipping rope
finishing point
route

*Figure 1*

# DOGGER

## Objective

RE – To develop an awareness that there are things in life which people value.

## Group size

Any size.

## What you need

A copy of the story *Dogger* by Shirley Hughes (Red Fox), red sugar paper, a pen that writes in gold ink, white drawing paper, gold paint, a small heart-shaped sponge, pencils, wax crayons, a stapler.

## Preparation

Cut two large heart shapes from the red sugar paper. Cut heart shapes of the same size from the white paper, making sure there is one for each child.

## What to do

Read the story *Dogger* to the children. When Dave loses his favourite soft toy dog (Dogger), he is extremely upset. Dave finds Dogger for sale at the school fête, but another child buys him first. Dave's sister Bella saves the situation by swopping a teddy she has won for Dogger. Discuss the story with your group and then talk about the special things which the children value.

Explain that they are going to make a book to show everyone's special things. Give each child a white heart shape and ask them to draw themselves with their special thing on it, and write a label next to the picture. Ask one child also to draw and label Dave with Dogger to go on the first page of the book.

Use the gold pen to write 'Special things' as a title on one of the red hearts. Ask two children to decorate both red hearts by sponge-printing small gold hearts on both sides of the paper using the gold paint. Assemble the book, using the red hearts as the front and back covers, and staple along the top (see Figure 1).

Put the finished book in the reading corner for the children to look at.

Figure 1

## Discussion

Talk about the relationship between Dave and his soft toy dog. What do they do together? How does Dave feel when the toy dog is lost and then bought by another child? Relate these feelings to people and real pets.

Invite the children to name a treasured possession and to say why it is important to them. It may be an old toy, a present given to them by someone important to them or a collection of natural objects such as stones or shells. How would they feel if they lost their special possession?

## Follow-up activities

✧ Discuss Bella's kind actions in the story.
✧ Ask children to mime actions of the characters as the story is read.
✧ Use play dough to make models of 'Dogger'.

# CHAPTER 2
# CATS

Cats are the subject of many popular early years fiction books. Stories, such as the *Mog* series by Judith Kerr (Picture Lions), are an ideal way of introducing this theme. Cats are also a rich source of inspiration for other areas of the curriculum such as poetry, drama, art and dance.

## CAT DRAWINGS

### Objective

Art – To draw cats based on first-hand observations.

### Group size

Any size.

### What you need

A real cat, pictures of different breeds of cat, oil pastels, pieces of grey and beige sugar paper in different sizes.

### What to do

Invite a cat owner to bring a cat into the nursery. Talk about the physical characteristics of the cat. Name body parts and describe its colour, shape and texture. Compare and contrast the real cat with the pictures of cats.

Tell the children that they are going to draw a cat with oil pastels. Ask them to choose the colour and size of the paper they will use. Remind them to fill most of the sheet with their drawing. Encourage them to mix colours by overlapping or blending them with their fingers. Mount and display the finished drawings.

### Discussion

As the children draw, encourage them to include as many physical characteristics as possible. How many claws will each paw have? Will the cat have a long or short coat? Are the whiskers straight or curved?

Talk about ways of making the drawn cat look furry, and highlight different methods that are being used. For example, children may draw short, straight lines or long, wavy lines and smudge them with their fingers to give a softer appearance.

Discuss the finished drawings on display. Count different body parts or the numbers of cats with particular colours. Which cat has the most interesting coat and why?

### Follow-up activities

✧ Ask each child to choose a cat from the display and to say why they would like to own it.
✧ Fill a feely bag with soft and hard objects. Ask individuals to identify the objects by touch.
✧ Compare and contrast various cat illustrations in picture books by authors such as Nicola Bayley and Ruth Brown.

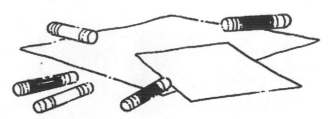

# WHAT'S MISSING?

## Objective

Science — To name the body parts of a cat.

## Group size

Small groups of up to six children.

## What you need

A large sheet of coloured sugar paper, a large sheet of white drawing paper, felt-tipped pens, scissors, PVA adhesive, Blu-Tack.

## Preparation

On the large sheet of white paper, draw and colour a large simple picture of a cat. Cut it out and then cut up the main body parts (head, body, legs, tail, ears). Stick the 'body' on to the coloured paper and use Blu-Tack to stick the other body parts in position.

## What to do

Show the children the picture of the cat you have made and name each body part. Ask them to close their eyes while you remove and hide one body part. Can they identify what's missing? Invite a child to stick the missing part back on to the picture.

Repeat this activity, initially removing one part at a time and then removing several. You could also allow a child to choose which parts to remove.

## Discussion

Talk about the shape of each body part and count legs, eyes, ears, tail, and so on. Ask the children to describe the exact position of each body part. What kind of movements can each body part make?

## Follow-up activities

✧ Use photocopiable sheet 89, which requires children to draw in the missing body parts on pictures of cats.
✧ Mount pictures of cats (from magazines or calendars) on card and cut them up to make simple puzzles.
✧ Read the poem 'Cats' on page 67 of the Resources section.

## CAT CARE LEAFLETS

### Objective

RE – To identify the key aspects of 'caring' for a cat.

### Group size

Any size for discussion, but small groups of up to six children for writing.

### What you need

A display board covered in dark blue backing paper, a child's drawing of a cat, a stapler, large hand shapes cut from light blue paper, a black felt-tipped pen, examples of pet care leaflets (often available free from vets), A4 writing paper, pencils, crayons, drawing pins.

### Preparation

Staple the child's drawing of a cat in the middle of the display board.

### What to do

Gather the group around the display board and invite the child who drew the cat to name it. Ask the group to pretend the cat is their pet and to say what they would need to do to care for it properly. As each new suggestion is made, write it on one of the paper hand shapes. Staple the hand shapes in place to make a border around the picture of the cat.

Show the children the pet care leaflets and discuss their design. Invite the children to write their own leaflets about caring for a cat. An adult can act as scribe for very young children. Pin the finished leaflets around the cat on the display board. Allow the children to remove the leaflets and read them if they wish to.

### Discussion

Encourage the children to consider both the physical needs (food, drink, shelter, warmth, health) and the emotional needs (play, affection, consistency of care) of the cat.

Use the examples of pet care leaflets to help the children decide on the design of their own leaflet. How will they fold their paper? Will they write on both sides? An adult can act as scribe for younger children. What information will they include? Remind them to look at the display for inspiration. What pictures will they draw?

### Follow-up activities

✧ Compare caring for a cat with caring for humans. Do all the points recorded on the hand shapes also apply to us?
✧ Invite someone to talk to the children from a pet care organisation such as the RSPCA, or local dog or cat rescue homes.
✧ Sing 'Pets Need Looking After' (see page 87 of the Resources section).

# CAT MASKS

● ● ● ● ● ● ● ● ● ● ● ● ● ● ● ● ● ● ● ● ● ● ● ● ● ● ● ● ● ● ● ●

## Objective
Technology – To make a mask.

## Group size
Small groups of up to six children.

## What you need
Pictures of different breeds of cat, six white paper plates, tissue paper (black, white, brown), PVA adhesive, glue sticks, scissors, sugar paper (black, white, brown), thick elastic bands.

## Discussion
Talk about which features are the same on each cat (two eyes, two ears, one nose) and which are different (colour, shape, texture).

As the children work, encourage them to describe their cat's face. Will it have a shaggy coat or a smooth coat? Is it more than one colour?

Assess the finished masks. Discuss how well they fit, whether the children can see through the eye holes adequately and whether they are pleased with the various features. Is there anything they would change next time?

## What to do
Look closely at the faces of the cats in the pictures to remind the children of the important features of a cat's face.

Give each child a paper plate and help them to mark and cut out the eye holes. Allow each child to choose some coloured tissue paper, then show them how to tear it into short strips and stick it all over the paper plate, avoiding the eye holes.

Cut the sugar paper to make ears, whiskers, a nose and a mouth and stick these on to the tissue paper. When the adhesive is dry, help each child to make a hole in each side of the mask and tie on some elastic to hold the mask in place.

## Follow-up activities
✧ Use the masks for drama and movement sessions (see the following activity) or when singing 'Naughty Little Kitten' (see page 86 of the Resources section).
✧ Make a collection of animal masks and compare and contrast their design.

# CAT MOVEMENTS

◆◆◆◆◆◆◆◆◆◆◆◆◆◆◆◆◆◆◆◆◆◆◆◆◆◆◆◆◆

## Objective

PE – To use movement to imitate the moods and feelings of a cat.

## Group size

Any size.

## What you need

A large open space, a tambourine, a xylophone.

## What to do

Invite the children to respond with movements to the following ideas; use percussion instruments to indicate the length of time they should move.

| Movement | Percussion suggestions |
|---|---|
| Creeping silently after a mouse. | Shake tambourine, pause sometimes. |
| Running after and pouncing on a mouse. | Shake tambourine, bang for pounce. |
| Patting and playing with leaves. | Shake tambourine. |
| Hissing and clawing angrily at a dog. | Shake and tap tambourine. |
| Climbing a tree. | Play low to high on xylophone. |
| Cleaning and grooming fur. | Slide beater up and down xylophone. |
| Stretching and yawning. | Slide beater up and down xylophone. |
| Curling up to sleep. | Play high to low on xylophone. |

## Discussion

Encourage the children to use the whole floor space when moving and to explore contrasts such as high and low, fast and slow. Ask one or two children to demonstrate their movements and then encourage the other children to suggest words to describe them. Invite the children to suggest alternative cat movement activities and percussion sounds.

## Follow-up activities

✧ Invite a child to mime cat movements and ask the others to guess what the cat is doing.
✧ Write a poem based on cat movements.
✧ Read the poems 'Black Cat' and 'Pet Fingers' on pages 69 and 71 of the Resources section.

# CAT RHYMES

• • • • • • • • • • • • • • • • • • • • • • • • • • •

## Objective

English – To develop an awareness of rhyming words.

## Group size

Any size.

## What you need

A display board covered in bright backing paper, white paper, paints, scissors, a stapler, a black felt-tipped pen.

## Preparation

Ask a child to paint a picture of a cat without a tail. When this is dry, cut it out and staple it to the display board. Cut some paper into rectangles (of a suitable size to make up the cat's tail, and large enough to write a word on each (see illustration).

## Discussion

Make sure the children understand about rhyming words by running through several different examples with them. Can they find lots of words that rhyme with 'cat' to make the tail as long as possible? What do the children notice about the last two letters in all of their rhyming words? Continue the activity over several days if appropriate.

## Follow-up activities

◇ Make up sentences using the words on the tail. For example, 'The fat cat sat on the hat.'
◇ Read poems and nursery rhymes about cats and ask the children to identify the rhyming words.
◇ Read the joining-in story 'Drat that Fat Cat!' on page 74 of the Resources section.

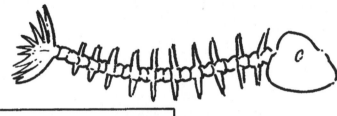

## What to do

Gather the children round the display and ask them to identify what's missing on the cat picture. Explain that they are going to help make the cat's tail out of words which rhyme with 'cat'. As the children suggest rhyming words, write each one on a rectangle-shaped piece of paper. To separate the words, draw a black stripe at the right-hand side of each rectangle. Staple the words in place to form a tail for the cat.

# DICK WHITTINGTON

## Objective

History — To develop an awareness of the past through the traditional story of Dick Whittington.

## Group size

Any size.

## What you need

A simple version of the story of 'Dick Whittington' (such as *Dick Whittington, Favourite Tales* series, Ladybird), drawing paper, pencils, wax crayons.

## What to do

Read the story to the group and talk about the illustrations. Briefly tell the story again, using the illustrations as a basis. At key points in the story, stop and ask the children to imagine how the cat is feeling. Talk about the reasons for the cat's feelings.

Give each child a sheet of paper and ask them to fold their paper in half. Invite them to draw, in each section, a picture of the cat at a different stage in the story and to write a sentence there explaining the cat's feelings. An adult can act as scribe for very young children.

## Discussion

After reading the whole story, ask the children to say how we know the story took place a long time ago. Encourage them to look for clues in the pictures and text and make comparisons with the present day. Are the people wearing clothes which we would wear today? Do we call people merchants, and pay for things with caskets of gold and jewels? Talk about whether the story is true or not.

Ask individual children to show and talk about their finished pictures. Can the group decide whether the pictures show the cat at the beginning, middle or end of the story?

## Follow-up activities

✧ Use the story as a basis for drama.
✧ Invite the children to use construction toys to build a boat for Dick Whittington's cat to sail in.
✧ Collect a variety of coloured foil papers (kitchen foil, sweet papers) and make a shiny necklace for Dick Whittington to wear as Lord Mayor.
✧ Use play dough to make mice and display these alongside a soft toy cat. Invite individuals to count the mice, removing some from the display each time to alter the total counted.

ACTIVITIES

# CLASSICAL CATS

## Objective

Music – To listen to a short piece of classical music and use it to inspire simple compositions.

## Group size

Any size.

## What you need

'The Cat Duet' (*Duetto Buffo di due gatti*) by Rossini, a tape recorder.

## What to do

Play 'The Cat Duet' by Rossini and ask the children to listen carefully to identify the animal sounds in the music. How many cats can the children hear? Help them to realise that the cats are having a conversation. Replay short sections of the duet and ask the children to describe how each cat is singing 'meow'.

Suggest that the children work in pairs and say or sing 'meow' to each other to form their own 'cat conversation'. Ask two or three pairs to perform to the group or record the duets on tape.

## Discussion

Explain that a duet involves two people and ask the children to listen carefully to identify the two voices. Talk about how each cat sings. Are they singing high, low, fast, slow, loud or soft? What

kind of emotions are conveyed in their conversation? Are they happy, sad, angry or afraid? Remind the children to consider these aspects when they compose their own musical 'conversation'.

Talk about the final performances of the children's duets. Which were the most successful and why?

## Follow-up activities

✧ Ask pairs of children to compose a conversation with percussion instruments. When they are satisfied with their composition, invite the children to record it on tape.
✧ Learn the traditional song 'Pussy cat, pussy cat, where have you been?' from *Over and Over Again* (Beaver Books) or *Pudding and Pie* (OUP) and then choose individuals to sing the two parts of the conversation.
✧ Invite pairs of children to make up a conversation between animal puppets. Encourage the pairs to perform their conversation to a small group.
✧ Play percussion instruments behind a screen and ask the children to state the number of instruments being used. Can they name each instrument?

# CHAPTER 3
# GUINEA-PIGS

Guinea-pigs are members of the rodent family and provide an interesting contrast to dogs and cats. Several of the suggested activities (such as 'Guinea-pig menu', 'Cage design' and 'Weekly diary') will be more successful if a real guinea pig can be observed over several days. Keeping a guinea pig for a longer period also helps children to realise the importance of regular feeding, grooming and cleaning.

## GUINEA-PIG MENU

### Objective
Science — To discover which foods guinea-pigs prefer.

### Group size
Any size.

### What you need
A real guinea-pig (to be kept in the nursery for several days), a large piece of coloured sugar paper, small pieces of white drawing paper, pencils, wax crayons, scissors, adhesive, a black felt-tipped pen.

### What to do
Use the black pen to write 'Squeaky's menu' at the top of the coloured sugar paper. Ask a child to draw and colour a picture of Squeaky the guinea pig on a small piece of paper, then cut it out and stick it next to the title.

Show the children the menu and explain that they are going to use it to record everything that Squeaky eats. Ask a child to draw and label a picture of each type of food eaten, then cut it out and stick it on to the menu. Find out which types of foods to try feeding to the guinea-pig by looking at information books or pet care leaflets from a vet. Guinea-pigs are vegetarian and their diet could include corn, vegetables, fruit, bread, oats, hay and dandelion leaves. Try different foods over several days and record the ones Squeaky prefers.

### Discussion
Talk about the type of foods the guinea-pig prefers. Which food does it like best? Compare what a guinea-pig (vegetarian) eats with what is eaten by a cat or dog (carnivore). Encourage the children to observe how the guinea-pig eats. Does it use its front legs? How does it grind its food? Remind the children of the importance of giving guinea-pigs fresh food and removing any old uneaten food from the cage.

### Follow-up activities
✧ Put several examples of guinea-pig food on a tray and ask the children to look at and remember what is there. Cover the tray and remove one item of food. Can the children identify the missing food?
✧ Compare the teeth of a guinea-pig with those of a cat or dog. Guinea-pigs need to gnaw hard foods and sometimes need a gnawing block, because their teeth are constantly growing.
✧ Read the poem 'Barney and Fred' on page 71 of the Resources section.
✧ Use guinea-pig food for simple weighing activities. Is one apple heavier than one slice of bread? What balances with two carrots?

# CAGE DESIGN

## Objective

Technology – To evaluate the design of a guinea-pig cage.

## Group size

Any size.

## What you need

A guinea-pig cage, a black felt-tipped pen, a large piece of paper.

## Preparation

This activity will be more successful if children have watched a guinea-pig use the cage for several days. Encourage them to watch and see if the guinea-pig uses certain areas of the cage for different functions, such as eating or sleeping. Does the guinea-pig spend more time in one area than another? Is the guinea-pig happy and active or always huddled in one corner?

## What to do

Gather the children around the guinea-pig cage. Talk about the good and bad aspects of the cage design.

Divide the large piece of paper into two columns, and label one 'good points' and the other 'bad points'. Write the points suggested by the children in the appropriate column.

## Discussion

Talk about the things a guinea-pig would need in a home and assess how well the cage meets these needs. Points for discussion could include space, warmth, light, ventilation, safe materials, feeding and sleeping areas. At the end of the activity, decide whether there are more 'good' than 'bad' points on the list. How could the cage design be improved?

## Follow-up activities

✧ Draw a picture of the cage and label the materials used in its construction.
✧ Write a story about a guinea-pig that has an unsuitable cage (see illustration above). Talk about how the guinea-pig would feel and whether the story would have a happy or a sad ending.
✧ Sing 'Pets' (see page 81 of the Resources section).
✧ Use junk modelling materials to build a model of a guinea-pig cage.
✧ Devise a rota so that all the children have the opportunity to help clean out the guinea-pig cage. Talk about the reasons for keeping the cage clean.

# WEEKLY DIARY

## Objective

History — To record the behaviour of a guinea-pig at regular times over a week.

## Group size.

Any size.

## What you need

A real guinea-pig, a time chart, a pencil, a card clock-face, a real clock.

## Preparation

Make a time chart as shown in Figure 1. Allow enough space for the children to draw and label a picture in each box.

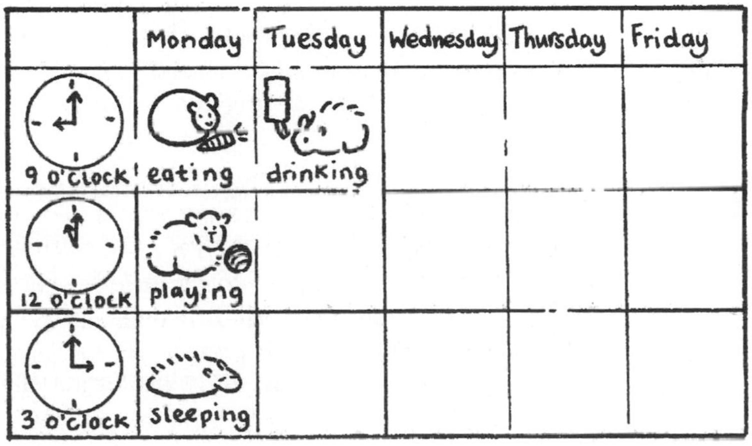

| | Monday | Tuesday | Wednesday | Thursday | Friday |
|---|---|---|---|---|---|
| 9 o'clock | eating | drinking | | | |
| 12 o'clock | playing | | | | |
| 3 o'clock | sleeping | | | | |

*Figure 1*

## What to do

Show the children the time chart. Explain that at certain times of the day, they are going to watch to see what the guinea-pig is doing and then take turns to draw a picture on the chart to show this. Continue recording on the chart for at least a week.

Very young children may find it helpful to have a card clock-face set at the time the guinea-pig is next to be observed. They can then compare it with the real clock to see when the times match.

## Discussion

Talk about what the guinea-pig is doing at each set time and compare the activities for each day. Is the guinea-pig feeding at the same time each day? On which days did the guinea-pig sleep? Look for a pattern in the guinea-pig's behaviour.

## Follow-up activities

✧ Cut the time chart into strips for days of the week, muddle them up and ask the children to sequence them correctly.

✧ Continue recording the guinea-pig's behaviour for more than one week and compare the results. Look for any patterns in behaviour.

✧ Suggest that the children make a similar diary chart for themselves over a week. At the end of the week, look at the chart to see if they are doing certain activities at regular times.

✧ Write a story about a guinea-pig who escapes on Monday and is found on Friday. Draw pictures to show what happens on each day (see Figure 2).

| Monday | Tuesday | Wednesday | Thursday | Friday |
|---|---|---|---|---|
| Squeaky escapes | squeaky gets wet | Squeaky finds food | Squeaky feels lonely | Squeaky is found |

*Figure 2*

# CLAY GUINEA-PIGS

## Objective

Art – To use clay to make a model of a guinea pig.

## Group size

Small groups of up to six children.

## What you need

A real guinea-pig, pictures of guinea-pigs, clay, small modelling boards, found materials (sticks, lollipop sticks, matchsticks, straws, a comb, screws) or modelling tools, straw bedding, hessian, three cardboard boxes (each a different size).

## What to do

Allow the children enough time to become familiar with the appearance and habits of the guinea-pig and to study the pictures. Talk about its physical characteristics and name body parts.

Give each child a modelling board and a lump of clay. Encourage them to pat and roll the clay into a ball shape. Squeeze out a head, two ears and four small legs. Use the found materials or the tools to add features such as eyes, a nose, whiskers and fur.

Allow the models to dry and then display them. Place the cardboard boxes on a table and drape them with hessian. Add some straw bedding and arrange the clay guinea-pigs on it. If you have access to a kiln, hollow out the guinea-pig models (from the bases) before drying and firing.

## Discussion

Encourage the children to use their observations of the real guinea-pig and the pictures as the basis for their modelling. Have they included all the body parts on their models?

Emphasise the need to squeeze, pull or pinch the clay rather than trying to stick other pieces on. Identify which tools are best for making the shapes or textures needed. Observe the change in colour and texture as the clay dries out.

## Follow-up activities

✧ Each day, allow a child to rearrange the model guinea-pigs on the bedding. Emphasise the need to handle the models carefully.
✧ Use the models for counting activities. How many eyes are there on three guinea-pigs? How many legs are there on two guinea-pigs?
✧ Make a collection of guinea-pig models or items with pictures of guinea-pigs on them. Identify the materials used to make each model or item (plastic, plaster, paper, fabric) and discuss which ones the children like or dislike.

# LOST AND FOUND

## Objective

RE – To explore the emotions associated with being lost.

## Group size

Small groups of up to six children.

## What you need

A model of a guinea-pig (you could use a clay model from the previous activity), six pieces of white paper, pencils, crayons, a black felt-tipped pen, a display board.

## What to do

Show the children the model guinea-pig and explain that it has escaped from its cage and is wandering around the room, lost and looking for home. Place the model guinea-pig somewhere in the room (behind a cupboard, in a toy box, under the sink). Ask the children to describe how it would feel. Repeat this using six different places, the final one being back in its cage.

Ask each child to draw and colour the guinea-pig in one of the six situations. Add a speech bubble from the guinea-pig's mouth and write its thoughts inside it. An adult can act as scribe for young children.

Display the pictures in sequence to show the six different places the guinea-pig visited in the room.

## Discussion

Encourage the children to identify with the guinea-pig's emotions. What would make it afraid? Suggest the children look at the room from the guinea-pig's viewpoint to discover frightening things such as the noise or the size of people and furniture. How does it feel to be lost? What would the guinea-pig miss most about its home?

## Follow-up activities

◇ Invite the children to describe occasions when they have been lost and discuss ways of obtaining help safely.
◇ Read the Biblical story *The Lost Sheep* by Nick Butterworth and Mick Inkpen (Marshall Pickering).
◇ Give the children photocopiable sheet 90 and ask them to join the dots to take each guinea-pig home.
◇ Read the story *Schnitzel von Krumm's Basketwork* by L. Dodd (see Recommended Materials list, page 96), and use the story to introduce a discussion about pets and their feelings.

# SIZES

### Objective

Mathematics — To identify animals larger and smaller than a guinea-pig.

### Group size

Small groups of up to six children.

### What you need

A guinea-pig, two large sheets of sugar paper (in different colours), felt-tipped pens, small pieces of white drawing paper, pencils, crayons, PVA adhesive, spreaders.

### What to do

Show the children the guinea-pig and ask each one to name an animal which is smaller. Draw a large set ring on one of the large pieces of paper and label it 'smaller than a guinea-pig'. Ask each child to draw and label a picture of their animal and to place it inside the set ring. Repeat the activity with the other large piece of paper, but this time look for animals 'larger than a guinea-pig'. Very young children may need an adult to act as scribe when labelling their pictures.

Play a game with the two sets of pictures. Ask the children to close their eyes while you swap over two pictures. Can they identify which animals are now in the wrong sets? At the end of the game, stick the pictures in the correct sets and display them.

### Discussion

As the children draw their pictures, encourage them to compare their animal with a guinea-pig. Does it have the same number of legs, ears, eyes? Does it have the same skin covering? Identify the smallest and largest animals that the children have drawn.

Encourage individuals to ask the group questions about the final display. For example, 'To which set does the dog belong?'

### Follow-up activities

✧ Invite a child to choose an animal from either set and to say why they would like to be that size.
✧ Sing 'John Brown had a little guinea-pig' (in *Over and Over Again*, Beaver Books). Invent other verses for animals larger or smaller than a guinea-pig.
✧ Draw three different animals (including a guinea-pig) in order of size.
✧ Read the poem 'Guinea Pigs' on page 69 of the Resources section.

# FOR SALE

## Objective

English – To develop listening and memory skills.

## Group size

Any size.

## What you need

An area for the children to sit in.

## What to do

Gather the children together, sitting in a group. Tell them that a guinea-pig is for sale and they are going to help describe it in great detail. Choose one child from the group and ask him to say 'I am a guinea-pig and I have ....', adding one attribute of his own (two black eyes, small ears, a loud squeak). Choose a second child and invite her to stand beside the first child. Ask her to repeat what the first child said and to add another attribute of her own. If a child is unable to remember the sequence correctly, she sits down again and another child is chosen. Continue the game for as long as is desired.

It is useful for the children to stand in sequence to help jog their memories. More experienced children may be able to memorise the sequence without the physical prompt.

## Discussion

Emphasise the need to find a different attribute each time and to describe it as fully as possible.

## Follow-up activities

✧ Invite each child to write her own 'For Sale' advertisement. An adult can act as scribe for very young children.
✧ Collect pet advertisements from a local paper. Read them to the group and discuss the information they contain. Ask the children to say which pet they would buy and why.
✧ Put a pretend cage and a soft toy guinea-pig in the home corner to stimulate role play and language.

# SQUEAK, GUINEA-PIG, SQUEAK

## Objective

Music – To develop listening skills and the ability to discriminate between loud and soft sounds.

## Group size

Any size.

## What you need

A blindfold.

## What to do

Ask the group to stand in a circle and choose one child to be blindfolded. Stand the child in the middle of the circle. Explain that the children in the circle are going to pretend to be guinea-pigs and that if they are touched by the child in the middle, they have to squeak. The blindfolded child then tries to recognise the voice. If she is successful, she swaps places with the child making the squeak. If not, she touches another child.

Extend the activity by asking the child in the middle to tell the child they are touching to 'squeak loudly' or 'squeak softly'.

## Discussion

Talk about the need for the blindfolded child to listen carefully and for the rest of the group to be silent. Is it easier to identify some people than others?

## Follow-up activities

✧ Repeat the activity, but change the instructions 'loud or soft' to 'fast or slow' or 'high or low'.
✧ Make a collection of squeaky toys and see if the children can identify them by sound alone.
✧ Record some guinea-pig noises on tape and compare them. Describe how the guinea-pig is squeaking and what it could mean.
✧ Read the poem 'Who Took the Cheese?' on page 68 of the Resources section.

# CHAPTER 4
# FISH

Access to an aquarium or tropical fish tank will be useful for providing first-hand observations of these pets. If it is difficult to arrange to bring an aquarium into the nursery, try visiting pet shops, zoos or garden centres with water garden departments.

## FISHY WORDS

### Objective

English – To develop descriptive vocabulary.

### Group size

Small groups of up to six children.

### What you need

An aquarium with fish, coloured paper fish shapes, a felt-tipped pen, a large sheet of blue sugar paper, green tissue paper, PVA adhesive, glue sticks, large sheets of white paper.

### What to do

Allow the children time to observe the fish. Encourage them to find words to describe the movements (diving, wiggling, gliding) and the physical characteristics (striped, golden, gleaming) of the fish. As each word is suggested, write it on a paper fish shape. Draw a large oblong on the sugar paper to represent the aquarium and stick the fish shapes on to this. Tear tissue paper and stick it on to serve as water weeds.

### Discussion

Ask the children questions to draw out more interesting descriptive words. What shape are the fish? How are they moving? Do they have any patterns on them?

Use the words collected as inspiration for a simple group poem. For example, start the poem with 'Fish are ...' and ask individual children to choose two words from the aquarium picture and put them together – for example, 'red and gleaming', 'wiggling and waggling' or 'bright and striped'. Write the chosen phrases as a poem on a large piece of paper. An adult can act as scribe for young children. Display the group poem next to the aquarium picture.

### Follow-up activities

✧ Play 'Find the Fish'. Ask individual children to point to the fish shape that shows a particular word or one whose word starts with a specified initial sound.

✧ Use the aquarium picture as a word bank when the children are writing about fish.

✧ Change the words of the song 'The Wheels on the Bus' to 'The fish in the tank .... swim up and down' or '...wiggle their fins' or '... blow big bubbles'.

# FISH PATTERNS

● ● ● ● ● ● ● ● ● ● ● ● ● ● ● ● ● ● ● ● ● ● ● ● ● ● ● ●

## Objective

Art – To explore patterns.

## Group size

Small groups of up to 6 children.

## Preparation

Use photocopiable sheet 91 to remind the children about colour and shape patterns.

## What you need

Tropical fish or pictures of tropical fish, white cartridge paper, paints, paintbrushes, palettes, water-pots, scissors, coloured chalks, a display board covered in blue backing paper.

## What to do

Talk about the tropical fish (or pictures of them), drawing attention to their size, shape and colour. Discuss any patterns which appear on them, such as alternate-coloured stripes (red, blue, red, blue).

Draw attention to the way that all patterns repeat themselves consistently.

Ask the children to paint a large fish on the white paper. Suggest that they colour it completely, using large different-coloured stripes. Allow the painting to dry and then cut it out. Invite the children to use the coloured chalks to draw patterns on to the painted stripes. Mount the fish on the display board.

## Discussion

Talk about the importance of allowing the paint to dry before using the chalks on the fish.

Refer the children back to the real fish (or pictures) for ideas on different types of patterns. Also remind them of handwriting patterns (zigzags, curved lines) and plane shapes (circles, squares, rectangles, triangles). Encourage them to check that their patterns repeat correctly.

## Follow-up activities

✧ Make a collection of patterned papers or fabrics and use them to make an underwater collage.
✧ Draw a dead fish (bought fresh from a fishmonger's) from observation. (Be aware of safety/hygiene considerations.)

# FISHING GAME

### Objective

Mathematics – To reinforce plane shape recognition.

### Group size

Two children.

### What you need

Coloured card, felt-tipped pens, scissors, paper-clips, two short pieces of bamboo, two pieces of string, two magnets.

### Preparation

Cut ten fish shapes (approximate size 20cm × 12cm) out of the coloured card. Divide them into pairs. On one side, decorate each pair of fish with the same plane shape (circles, triangles, squares, oblongs, hexagons). Put a paper-clip on to the mouth of each fish.

Make a simple fishing rod by attaching the magnet to the string and the string to the piece of bamboo.

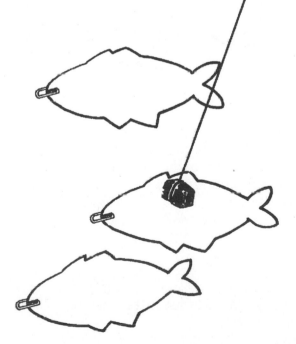

### What to do

Place the fish (decorated side down) on the floor. Give each child a rod and ask them to take turns to catch a fish with the magnet. Each child keeps the first fish she catches and then tries to find its partner. If she catches a fish which does not match the first one, she returns it (decorated side down) to the floor. If she catches a fish which does match, she keeps it and catches another one to start searching for a new pair. (Fish caught can be shown to all the group.) The game ends when all the fish have been caught.

### Discussion

Ask the children to name the plane shapes on the fish. Which fish are they trying to catch? At the end of the game, count the matching pairs and identify the shapes.

### Follow-up activities

✧ Invite the children to make their own pairs of fish for the game, using numbers or letters.
✧ Using photocopiable sheet 92, ask the children to colour the fish with more than two spots (or another number). Alternatively, the children could be asked to colour the fish with less than five spots (or another number).
✧ Make two copies of photocopiable sheet 92 and use it to make a fishing game. Play the game as outlined above, but ask the children to find pairs of fish with matching spots.

# FLOATING AND SINKING FISH

## Objective

Science — To investigate floating and sinking.

## Group size

Small groups (four to six children).

## What you need

A water tray, orange and yellow balloons, felt-tipped pens (waterproof markers), orange and yellow Plasticine, two sets of rings.

## Preparation

Make the balloons into fish by blowing them up slightly and leaving a small 'tail' when tying a knot. For safety reasons, only adults should blow up the balloons, preferably using a balloon pump. Use the waterproof markers to draw eyes, a mouth, gills and fins on to the balloon.

Make fish shapes out of the Plasticine.

## What to do

Allow the children to play with the balloons and the Plasticine fish in the water tray. Warn the children that balloons sometimes burst and may startle them.

Invite the children to take each fish in turn, and then predict and test to see whether it will float or sink. Use the set rings to sort them into two sets according to whether they float or sink.

## Discussion

Talk about the similarities between all the fish that float. Encourage the children to push the balloon fish to the bottom of the tray, then release them and describe what happens. Discuss the similarities between all the fish that sink. Do they all sink to the bottom or only halfway?

## Follow-up activities

✧ Collect other fish-shaped objects (sponges, soaps, plastic toys) and add these to the water tray. Which ones float or sink?

✧ Listen to 'The Aquarium' from *Carnival of the Animals* by Saint-Saëns.

# FISH ALIVE!

## Objective

Music – To learn a simple song.

## Group size

A minimum of ten children.

## What you need

Ten card fish (use those made for 'Fishing game' on page 37), ten paper-clips, ten small pieces of paper, a black felt-tipped pen, the song 'One, two, three, four, five, Once I caught a fish alive' in *Sing Hey Diddle Diddle* (A & C Black).

## Preparation

Write the numbers 1 to 10 on the small pieces of paper and use a paper-clip to attach one number to each fish.

## What to do

Teach the children to sing the song and then ask them to invent some actions to accompany the words.

When they can sing and mime the actions well, introduce the numbered fish. Ask ten children each to choose a fish and then sit in a line. Suggest that they hold up their fish. Now invite the other children to help put these children in order according to the number on their fish. Once the children are sitting in the right order, sing the song again. As each number is sung, the child with that number holds up his fish. The children all drop their fish when they sing 'Then I let it go again'.

## Discussion

Talk about the need to match the actions to the words of the song. This is particularly important when the children are holding up their fish as each number is sung. Try singing the song at different speeds and discuss which speed allows enough time for the actions to be completed comfortably.

## Follow-up activities

✧ Make a number chart with fish drawn by the children (see Figure 1).

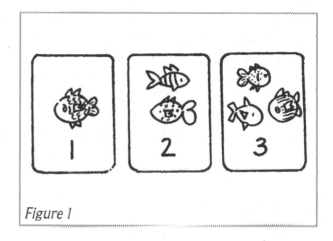

*Figure 1*

✧ Play 'Heads and tails'. Make card fish, and on each half of each fish write a number from 1 to 10 and the corresponding number of dots (see Figure 2). Cut the fish in half and invite the children to match the correct head to each tail.
✧ Collect music books and tapes with songs about fish on them. Find out which song in the collection is most popular, and learn it together.

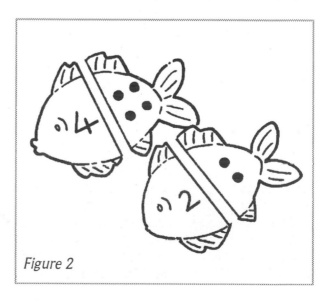

*Figure 2*

# FLAPPING FISH

## Objective

Technology — To use air to make a paper fish move.

## Group size

Small groups (up to six children).

## What you need

Six pieces of paper, pencils, crayons, scissors, white chalk, things to flap (such as pieces of card, paper fans, newspapers, large books, wooden bats).

## Discussion

Talk about what is making the fish move. Which object works best as a fan? Is there a particular way of holding or moving the fan that is more successful?

Ask the children to describe the movements of the paper fish. Does part or the whole of the fish lift up as it moves? Is the fish moving forwards in a straight line?

## Follow-up activities

✧ Have a race with the paper fish and reinforce place values by recording the order of the winners.
✧ Invite the children to make their own paper fans, choosing from a variety of different papers (tissue, newspaper, sugar paper, thin card). Talk about which fans work best and discuss the reasons for this.
✧ Make a list of things moved by the wind — smoke, washing, leaves, seeds, sailing boats.
✧ Sing 'Who am I?' (see page 85 of the Resources section).

## What to do

Invite the children to draw and colour a large fish on their piece of paper. Cut out the fish.

Use the chalk to draw a start and finish line on the floor. Ask the children to place their fish at the start line and move them to the finish line by fanning with one of the objects. Repeat this activity and encourage them to test out several different 'fanning' objects.

# GLOBE GAME

## Objective

Geography – To distinguish between areas of land and water on a globe.

## Group size

Small groups (up to six children).

## What you need

A globe on a stand, a blindfold.

## What to do

Talk about the globe in simple terms. Explain that it represents the Earth on which we live, and find Great Britain. Invite the children to find areas of water (sea, rivers, lakes) on the globe. Talk about the different colours used to represent water and land.

Make sure the children understand that fish live in water. Blindfold a volunteer and spin the globe. Ask the blindfolded child to use one finger to stop the globe and to keep their finger on that spot. Invite the group to decide whether a fish could live there. Repeat the activity, with different children taking turns to be blindfolded.

## Discussion

Find small areas of water on land (lakes and rivers) as well as large areas of water (oceans and seas). Is more of the Earth's surface land or water?

## Follow-up activities

✧ Use blue and green paint to paint large simple maps. When these are dry, allow the children to play with toys (small people, cars, boats, houses, animals, fish) on the maps, encouraging them to create realistic situations.
✧ Use upturned clay flowerpots (various sizes) to create areas of land in the water tray.
✧ Stick a maze of islands on to a large sheet of blue paper. Invite individual children to move a paper fish through the maze without touching the islands.

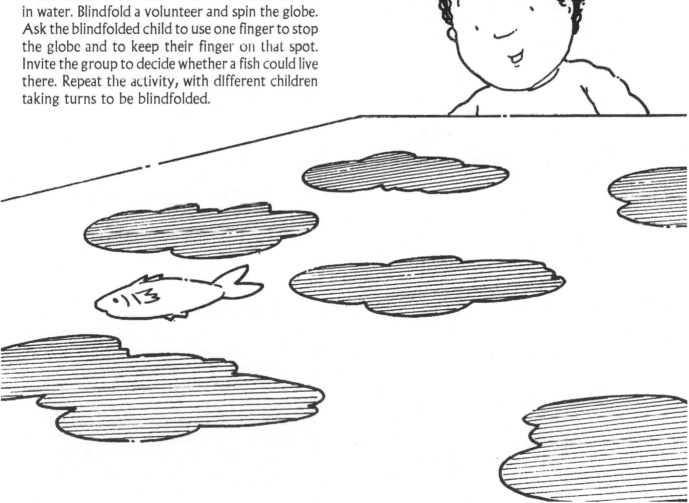

# SHARKS ABOUT!

## Objective

PE — To practise chasing and dodging in a simple game.

## Group size

Any size.

## What you need

Three or four PE mats, wooden claves, a large open space.

## What to do

Place the PE mats on the floor, spaced well apart. Explain that the mats represent the land and the floor is the sea. Tell the children they are going to go for a swim in the sea. Allow them to practise moving on two feet, making swimming movements with their arms, around the floor area.

Choose one child to be the shark and explain that when you tap the claves together (the shark's snapping teeth), the shark is going to try to catch the others. They must swim back to the dry land (PE mats). Any children who are caught also become sharks. Remove the mats one at a time as the game progresses, until only one is left. The game finishes when only two or three children remain uncaught.

## Discussion

Encourage the children to 'swim' around the whole floor space and not just to stay close to a mat. Emphasise the need to follow the rules of the game — sharks can only move when the claves are being tapped, a gentle touch of the hand is all that is needed to catch someone. Talk about why these rules are important to guarantee fairness and safety. Encourage the children to use dodging movements to avoid the sharks.

## Follow-up activities

✧ Create an obstacle course to represent the land. Any child touching the floor (the sea) while moving around the course is caught by a shark and thus eliminat ed.
✧ On a warm day, set up a paddling pool outdoors and suggest that the children pretend to be fish.
✧ Write a story about keeping a pet shark. Where would you keep it? What would it eat? Could you play with it? An adult could act as scribe for young children.

# CHAPTER 5
# RABBITS

Rabbits are another popular pet, and it should not prove too difficult to borrow one for the day or for a longer period. They also offer an opportunity to compare the life of a pet rabbit with that of a wild one. Look at differences in their feeding habits, the homes in which they live and their way of life.

## RABBIT DRAWINGS

### Objective

Art – To use Albrecht Dürer's drawing of 'The Hare' to inspire pencil drawings of rabbits.

### Group size

Small groups (up to six children).

### What you need

A copy of 'The Hare' by Albrecht Dürer (see *Art & Craft* magazine, January 1994), or alternatively use any drawing of a rabbit; a real rabbit, 6B pencils, white cartridge paper.

### What to do

Talk about Albrecht Dürer's picture. Explain that a hare is similar to a rabbit. Focus on the different types of line used to draw the hare. Allow the children time to look at the real rabbit and compare it to the picture of the hare.

Ask the children to make a pencil drawing of the rabbit from observation. Suggest that they try to include a variety of lines in the way that Dürer has.

Display the finished drawings alongside Dürer's picture.

### Discussion

Talk about the differences between a hare and a rabbit – a hare has longer ears with black tips, and larger back legs.

Find different types of line on the picture – long, short, curved, straight. Where have short straight lines been used? Encourage the children to use similar lines in their drawing of a rabbit.

Talk about the finished drawings. Identify which rabbits have a smooth coat and which ones have a fluffy coat. What kind of lines have been used to achieve this? Which rabbit would the children most like to touch and why?

### Follow-up activities

✧ Collect rabbit pictures and sort them into sets according to whether they are photographs, drawings, prints, and so on.
✧ Draw a picture of a rabbit in a sheet of clay, Plasticine or play dough. Experiment with tools and junk materials as drawing implements to achieve different types of line.
✧ Use information books to find out more about hares and rabbits.

# RABBIT PHONICS TABLE

## Objective

English – To find words with the same initial sound as 'rabbit'.

## Group size

Small groups (up to six children).

## What you need

A display board, a small table, dark blue sugar paper, two large pieces of beige sugar paper, felt-tipped pens, a stapler, adhesive, white cartridge paper, a soft toy rabbit, a short length of wool, yellow sugar paper cut into triangle shapes, a collection of objects (including some that begin with the letter 'r'), pencils, crayons.

## Preparation

Cover a display board and a small table with dark blue sugar paper. Draw two large pictures of a rabbit hutch on the beige sugar paper. Staple one to the display board and stick the other to the table. Draw a large simple picture of a rabbit on the white cartridge paper, cut it out and stick it on to the hutch on the display board. Stick a label with a large 'r' written on it on to the rabbit. Place a soft toy rabbit on the hutch on the table and tie a label with a large 'r' written on it around the rabbit's neck.

## What to do

Show the children both the rabbits in their hutches, pointing out the letter 'r' on each one. Remind the children how to form the letter correctly, and ask them to write it in the air. Give each child a yellow triangle shape, help them position it with the point downwards and ask them to draw a large letter 'r' on it. Very young children could join dots drawn by an adult. Stick the letters as a border around the edge of the display board and table.

Show the children the collection of objects and name each one. Explain that the toy rabbit will only allow objects beginning with the letter 'r' to be placed in its hutch. Ask individuals to help sort the objects, placing those beginning with 'r' on the picture of the hutch and any others on the blue paper around it.

Invite the children to find other objects beginning with 'r' to place on the hutch. Encourage them to look around the room or to bring things from home.

Point out the rabbit and hutch on the display board and explain that this rabbit will only allow *pictures* of things beginning with 'r' to be placed in its hutch. Suggest that they draw pictures of their own, or cut pictures from catalogues or magazines, of anything beginning with the letter 'r'. Write the name of each object on the picture and stick it on to the rabbit hutch on the display board.

## Discussion

Maintain the children's interest in the display by encouraging them to look at it for a few minutes each day. Can they identify any new objects or pictures which have been added to the display? Mix up the sets of objects and ask the children to put them back into the correct positions. Place objects and pictures of your own which do not begin with 'r' on the display and challenge the children to find the odd one out.

## Follow-up activities

✧ Reinforce this activity by using photocopiable sheet 93. Invite the children to make up sentences using as many of the 'r' words as possible.
✧ Play a memory game with the display. Ask the children to look carefully at the display for a few minutes and then to shut their eyes and name as many of the 'r' objects and pictures as possible.

# FUR, FEATHER, SCALES

## Objective

Science — To group pets according to their skin covering.

## Group size

Small groups (up to six children).

## What you need

A large sheet of white cartridge paper, a black felt-tipped pen, pencils, crayons, pictures of a variety of pets (including a rabbit).

## What to do

Show the children the picture of a rabbit and talk about its skin covering. Look at the other pictures of pets. Identify each pet and talk about the type of skin covering found on each one.

Display the large sheet of paper nearby. Draw three large rings and label one 'Fur', one 'Feather' and one 'Scales'. Ask individual children to choose a picture of a pet and say which ring it belongs to. When they have identified the correct ring, suggest that they draw a small picture of that pet, label it and place it inside the ring. An adult can act as scribe for young children. Repeat for each pet picture.

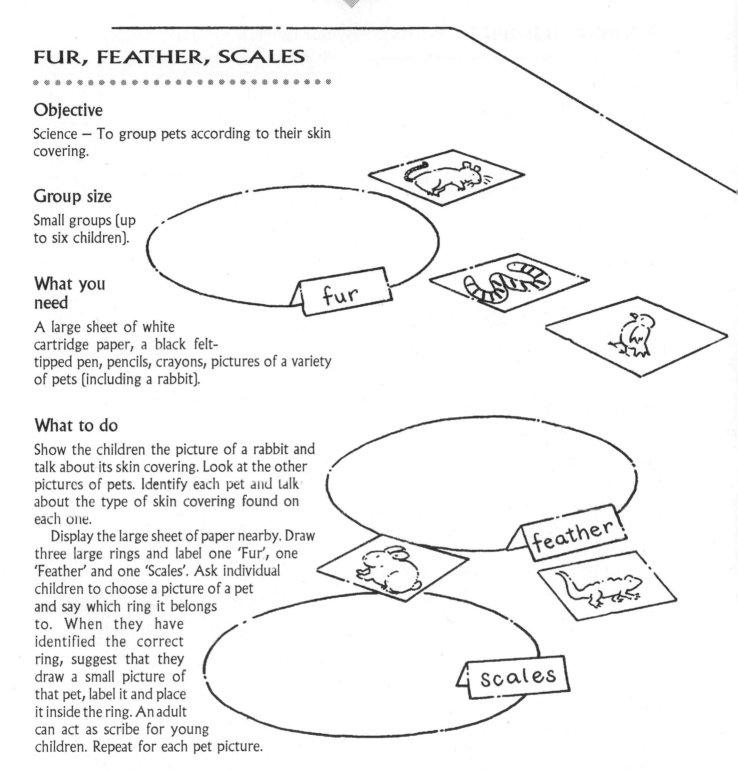

## Discussion

Talk about the purposes of skin covering (protection, sensory, temperature control) and identify reasons for each pet's type of skin covering. Is it the same all over the body? Are some parts bare? Look at the colour of the skin covering and talk about camouflage. Count the number of pets in each ring and find out which set has most / least.

## Follow-up activities

✧ Invite the children to sort small plastic zoo or farm animals according to skin covering.
✧ Ask the children to draw an animal which they would like to touch and then complete the following sentence: 'I would like to touch .... because ....' An adult can act as scribe for young children.
✧ Collect and draw different types of feather.

# RABBIT JUMPS

## Objective
PE — To practise different ways of jumping.

## Group size
Any size.

## What you need
Hoops, benches, mats, a large open space.

## Preparation
Arrange the hoops, benches and mats in a large open space.

## What to do
Warm up by asking the children to jump with feet together, first on the spot and then travelling, using the floor space in between the apparatus. Repeat this exercise, jumping with feet apart. Ask the children to find other ways of jumping using feet only.

Teach the children how to do bunny hops. Ask them to crouch down with two hands flat on the floor and kick their legs up behind them, keeping their feet together. Practise bunny hops first on the spot and then travelling. Ask the children to find other ways of jumping using hands and feet.

Invite them to explore different ways of jumping using the apparatus. Suggest that they try jumps with feet only to begin with, then try jumps with hands and feet.

## Discussion
Compare the way humans jump (using two feet) with rabbits (using four feet). Ask the children to describe which parts of the body they are using when jumping. Can they jump with two hands and one foot, or one hand and two feet? Discuss whether they are using the same or different ways of jumping on the different pieces of apparatus. Are they jumping over or on and off the apparatus?

## Follow-up activities
◇ List other animals which jump with two or four feet.
◇ Read and mime the action rhyme 'Jumping here, jumping there' (see page 73 of the Resources section).

# EASTER RABBITS

* * * * * * * * * * * * * * * * * * * * * * * * * *

## Objective

RE – To find out about Easter traditions.

## Group size

Small groups (up to six children).

## What you need

A hard-boiled egg for each child, felt-tipped pens.

## What to do

Tell the children the story about the Easter rabbit (originally a hare) leaving eggs in the garden for the children to find.

Explain that the children are going to decorate some hard-boiled eggs. Give each child an egg and ask them to use the felt-tipped pens to decorate the eggs with patterns and shapes. When they have finished, ask them to pretend to be Easter rabbits and to hide their eggs around the room (or outside if weather permits). Invite another group of children to find all the eggs.

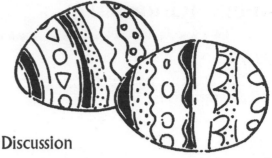

## Discussion

Talk about the decoration on each egg. What colours, shapes or patterns have been used?

Encourage the children to handle the eggs carefully and to put them in a safe hiding place. As the second group of children search for the eggs, the first group could give them clues. They can either say 'hot' or 'cold' according to how close a child is to an egg, or they could give more specific clues – 'It's near to something red,' 'It's in between the sand tray and the bricks,' and so on.

## Follow-up activities

◇ Make Easter rabbit head-dresses (see below).

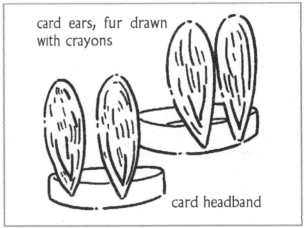

card ears, fur drawn with crayons

card headband

◇ Cook Easter rabbit biscuits.
*Ingredients:* 175g self-raising flour (sieved), 50g castor sugar, 125g margarine; 1 egg (separated), a few currants, extra castor sugar.
*What to do:* Mix the flour and sugar together. Rub in the margarine, then add the egg yolk with one or two teaspoons of water and knead to make a stiff dough. Roll out the dough thinly and use a rabbit-shaped pastry cutter to cut out the biscuits. Press in currant eyes, a nose and a tail. Beat the egg white until frothy, brush over the rabbits and sprinkle with castor sugar. Place on a greased baking tray and bake at 180°C (Gas mark 4, 350°F) for 10 to 15 minutes.

# RUNNING RABBITS

## Objective

Music – To experience fast and slow rhythms with percussion instruments.

## Group size

Any size.

## What you need

Three simple pictures (a rabbit, a fox and a burrow) on separate pieces of paper, percussion instruments (tambour, tambourine, maracas, claves, wood blocks).

## What to do

Sit the children in a circle and place the percussion instruments in the middle. Ask individual children to name each instrument and show how it is played.

Show the children the picture of the rabbit. Explain that the rabbit is hopping along at an even pace. Invite the children to play the percussion instruments (or tap their knees or clap their hands) to show this even pace. Help them to play together by asking them to follow the speed of your clapping.

Show the children the picture of the burrow. Explain that when the rabbit picture is held up, the children must play their instruments to show the rabbit hopping. However, when the burrow is held up, they must stop immediately because the rabbit has entered its burrow and gone to sleep. Practise holding up the pictures of the rabbit and burrow alternately.

When the children are proficient at responding to the two pictures, introduce the third picture: the fox. The fox is chasing the rabbit, so the rabbit must run very fast. When the fox picture is held up, the children must play their instruments very quickly.

## Discussion

Talk about playing the instruments quickly or slowly, and the need to stop when indicated. Is there a clear difference between the speeds used by the children at the different times?

## Follow-up activities

✧ Ask one child to play an instrument and another to say whether the music is slow or fast.
✧ Sing the song 'See the little bunny sleeping' in *This Little Puffin* (Young Puffin).

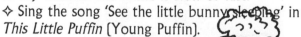

# ABOVE AND BELOW GROUND

• • • • • • • • • • • • • • • • • • • • • • • • • • • • • • • • •

## Objective

Geography – To identify animals living above and below ground.

## Group size

Any size.

## What you need

A display board, two long strips of white paper, sponges, blue and brown paint, small pieces of white cartridge paper, paints, paintbrushes, scissors, a stapler, white strips of paper for labels, felt-tipped pens, Blu-Tack.

## What to do

Sponge-print one strip of white paper blue and the other brown. When they are dry, staple them to the display board to represent the sky and under the ground. Label the sky area 'Above the ground' and the underground area 'Below the ground'.

Talk with the children about where wild rabbits would normally live. Then ask them to name other animals that live or have homes underground. These might include worms, moles, ants, badgers, foxes and mice. Write the name of each animal suggested on a label and ask a child to paint a small picture of that animal. Repeat this for animals living above the ground such as birds, hedgehogs, deer and ponies. When the pictures are dry, cut them out and ask each child to indicate where their animal should be placed on the display board and then to use Blu-Tack to stick the picture and label on to the correct strip (help where necessary).

## Discussion

Talk about the differences between the home of a pet and that of a wild rabbit. Why would a wild rabbit want its burrow to be underground? Discuss whether wild rabbits spend the whole or part of their lives below ground. As other animals are suggested for 'below ground', talk about their reasons for living there. These may include warmth, safety from predators, closeness to food sources and avoidance of light.

## Follow-up activities

✧ Swap some of the pictures over and ask the children to identify the animals in the wrong places.
✧ Discuss whether the children would prefer to be a wild or a pet rabbit.
✧ Sing 'The Rabbit's Warning' on page 84 of the Resources section.

# RABBIT COUNT

## Objective
Mathematics – To practise counting to ten accurately.

## Group size
Any size.

## What you need
White card, felt-tipped pens, scissors.

## Preparation
Draw five identical rabbits on the card. Make each rabbit roughly A4 size and make sure that the children can easily count all the body parts (see Figure 1). Colour the rabbits and cut them out.

*Figure 1*

## What to do
Hold up one card rabbit and help the children to count how many ears, legs and tails it has. Then hold up more than one card and ask the children to count the ears, legs or tails. Repeat this activity with a different number of cards each time, but keep the total number of body parts counted to ten or less.

When the children are confident with this activity, allow a child to choose the number of rabbits and the body part to be counted.

## Discussion
Name the body parts on the rabbit. Encourage the children to touch each body part as they count. Can the children suggest other body parts to count, such as noses or eyes?

## Follow-up activities
✧ Use photocopiable sheet 94 to reinforce counting and naming various body parts of a rabbit.
✧ Compare the number of various body parts on a human with those on a rabbit. Do we have two eyes and one tail, like a rabbit?
✧ Learn the action song 'Peter Rabbit' (to the tune of 'John Brown's Body'). Add other verses by changing the body part on which the fly lands.
*Peter Rabbit has a fly upon his nose*
(repeat three times)
*So he flicked and he flicked and the fly flew away.*

*Powder puffs and curly whiskers*
(repeat three times)
*So he flicked and he flicked and the fly flew away.*
✧ Play 'Rabbits Hiding'. Hide one or more card rabbits behind a bush-shaped piece of paper, leaving one body part showing (ears, feet or tail). Can the children say how many rabbits are hiding?

# CHAPTER 6
# THE PET SHOP

**A visit to a pet shop would be an ideal introduction to this theme. Even if the pet shop sells equipment and not animals, it would be a valuable experience. Supermarkets or garden centres with large pet care departments could also be visited.**

## THE PET SHOP

### Objective

Technology – To set up a pet shop in the nursery.

### Group size

Any size for discussion, but small groups of up to six children for the activities.

### What you need

An area suitable for setting up a shop, a large sheet of paper, a felt-tipped pen, real or home-made pet care items, soft toy pets, pictures of pets (use old calendars), a toy till, toy money, bags, paper and pencils.

### Preparation

Visit a pet shop. If possible, take photographs to remind the children about the layout and the items sold in the shop.

### What to do

Talk with the children about the things they would like to have in their pet shop. List their suggestions on the large sheet of paper and then tick off each suggestion as it is included in the shop.

Borrow real pet care items such as leads, collars, food containers, tinned food, grooming equipment and toys. Make pretend items such as cardboard bones or Plasticine biscuits.

Allow the children to arrange the furniture and pet care items in the shop. Use the pictures to decorate the shop, and write appropriate signs.

Invite the children to use the pet shop for role-play activities.

### Discussion

Discuss the goods and equipment needed in a pet shop with the children. Remind them of their visit to a pet shop, if this has been possible. What kind of furniture will be needed? Which pets and items of equipment will be sold? What signs and labels will be necessary? Talk about what things the customers will need to bring, such as purses, money and shopping bags.

Encourage the children to evaluate how well the shop works and whether any alterations need to be made to improve it. Is the till in an easily-accessible place? Should some of the goods be displayed in the window or outside the shop?

### Follow-up activities

✧ Design paper bags for use in the pet shop.
✧ Make cages, aquariums and hutches from small cardboard boxes.
✧ Sing 'Daddy Wouldn't Buy Me a Bow Wow' from *Apusskidu*, see page 96.

# PET MONEY

## Objective

Mathematics – To practise coin recognition.

## Group size

Small groups of up to six children.

## What you need

A 'pet shop' (see previous activity), small sticky labels, a felt-tipped pen, an example of each of the coins we use (or realistic plastic or cardboard coins), six set rings.

## Preparation

Use the small sticky labels to label each object for sale in the pet shop with a price. Use prices which correspond to specific coins – 1p, 2p, 5p, 10p, 20p, 50p, £1.

## What to do

Show the children the coins and identify the value of each one. Compare and contrast the different coins, considering colour, size, shape and the pictures and numbers on the coin faces.

Ask each child to choose a coin and to place it inside a set ring. Invite them to find goods in the pet shop with prices which match the value of their coin. Suggest that they place the goods inside their set ring. Talk about the goods they have found.

Repeat the activity with each child choosing a different coin.

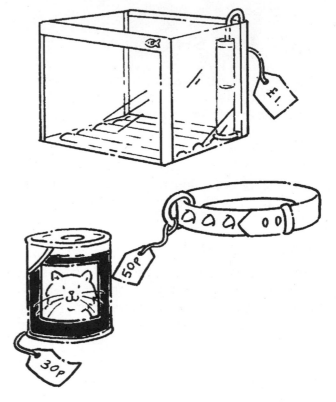

## Discussion

Count the number of coins which are silver or copper. Find the largest or smallest coin. Which coins are circle-shaped?

Encourage the children to look carefully at the price label on each item to see whether it matches their coin. How many items can they find for their coin?

## Follow-up activities

✧ Make rubbings of each coin.
✧ During role-play shopping sessions, ask an adult helper to sit at the till. Encourage the children to buy one item at a time, and to find the correct coin from their purse to match the price label.
✧ Read the poem 'Next Door's Dinosaur' on page 72 of the Resources section and use it to introduce a discussion about keeping more unusual pets.

# MATERIAL MUDDLES

## Objective

Science — To talk about materials and their properties.

## Group size

Small groups (up to six children).

## What you need

Pet care items made from a variety of materials (a metal comb, a plastic dish, a nylon or leather lead, a glass or plastic fish tank, a fabric cat basket), labels — some with the names of corresponding materials (metal, plastic, leather, glass, fabric) and some with incorrect names (wood, sponge, Plasticine, paper, cardboard).

## What to do

Sit the children in a circle. Place the pet care items in the middle of the circle with an incorrect label beside each one.

Invite individual children to choose a label, read it out and say whether it correctly describes the material of the object it is next to. Show the children the correct labels and ask them to choose the one which matches each object. Place the object and the corresponding label together. Throughout this activity, it would be best if there were an adult to help the children read the labels.

## Discussion

Talk about each incorrect label. Why would the material named be unsuitable for that object? What are the disadvantages of a paper lead or a card fish tank?

When the correct material has been identified, discuss its advantages. Why is plastic a more suitable material for a feeding dish than sponge or wood? Invite the children to name other objects in the room which are made from plastic. Can they suggest alternative materials for a feeding dish?

## Follow-up activities

✧ Invite the children to put together a display of objects made from one material.
✧ Describe a pet shop where everything is made from inappropriate materials — fish tanks made from ice, hutches from jelly and leads from Plasticine.

## OLD AND NEW

### Objective

History — To distinguish between old and new objects.

### Group size

Any size.

### What you need

Two examples (one new and one old) of each of three or four pet care items (a lead, a dog chew, a grooming brush, a pet toy), two sorting hoops, two labels (one for 'old' and one for 'new').

### What to do

Place the hoops on the floor with a label inside each one. Read the labels with the children.

Show the group one pair of objects. Compare and contrast the old and new objects. Ask the children to identify which object is older. Place each object in the correct hoop. Repeat this activity with each pair of objects.

### Discussion

Talk about the purpose of each object and look for signs of ageing. Has the object been scratched or worn? Are there signs of use, such as teeth marks or hairs? How can we tell which object is older?

### Follow-up activities

✧ Display the objects with a detailed written description of each one. Mix up the objects and descriptions and ask the children to match them correctly.
✧ Write a story about a pet that preferred its old bed to a brand new one.
✧ Invite the children to bring in items to make a collection of favourite old things. These could include clothes, toys and books. Talk about the collection and ask each child to explain why a particular old object is their favourite.

# PET SHOP MATCH

• • • • • • • • • • • • • • • • • • • • • • • • • • • • • • • •

## Objective

Geography – To introduce the idea that different shops sell different goods.

## Group size

Small groups (up to six children).

## What you need

Three plastic storage crates, items which would be sold in a pet shop (a lead, a comb, a packet of dog biscuits, a rubber bone), items to represent two other distinctive types of shops (for example, a potato, a carrot, an apple and an orange for a greengrocer's shop; a jumping beetle, a teddy, a car and a boat for a toy shop), a picture label representing each shop, a large cardboard box.

## Preparation

Place the three storage crates upside down in the carpet area, and stick a picture label on each one to represent the three different shops. Put all of the items into a large cardboard box nearby.

## What to do

Tell the children that each upturned crate represents a shop, and ask them to deduce what kind of shop each one stands for from the label. Show them the items in the cardboard box and tell them that these have all been muddled up. Ask the children to help you deliver the goods to the appropriate shops. Allow each child to choose one item at a time and then place it on the upturned crate representing the correct shop. When all the items have been correctly allocated, allow the children a period of free play to 'shop'.

## Discussion

As each item is removed from the cardboard box, discuss it with the children. What is it? Who would use it? Have the children ever seen it (or something similar in a shop)? Which type of shop would you buy it from? Once all the items have been correctly allocated to a shop, talk about the shops with the children. Have they ever been to a pet shop? What else would you buy in a greengrocer's shop? What other shops are the children familiar with?

## Follow-up activities

✧ On photocopiable sheet 95, ask the children to draw a mapping arrow to join each item to the appropriate shop.
✧ Visit a vet's surgery and use it as inspiration for setting up a role-play area in the nursery.
✧ Sing 'Come to the Pet Shop' (see page 84 of the Resources section).

# PET MOVEMENTS

## Objective

PE – To experience different ways of moving.

## Group size

Any size.

## What you need

A large open space.

## What to do

Explain that the children are going to move like different kinds of pet. Suggest pets and appropriate movements of your own, then ask the children for ideas. The following pets could be included:

| | |
|---|---|
| Dog | Moving quickly on all fours. |
| Cat | Slow stretched movements on all fours. |
| Rabbit | Bunny hops, fast and slow. |
| Snake | Wriggling and slithering along the ground. |
| Pony | Trotting with knees high. |
| Budgie | Running on tiptoes, flapping wings, high to low. |
| Tortoise | Plodding slowly on all fours. |
| Fish | Gliding on tiptoes, high to low. |

## Discussion

Encourage the children to use the whole of the floor space when moving, and to avoid touching others. Remind them to move in different directions: sideways, forwards and backwards.

Invite the children to think of alternative movements for the pets you suggest. Encourage them to base their movement ideas on any first-hand observations of pets.

## Follow-up activities

✧ Play 'Follow My Leader'. Invite one child to choose a pet movement and ask the others to follow in a line, copying the first child.
✧ List words to describe pet movements: creep, prowl, slither, hop, and so on.
✧ Choose percussion instruments to accompany the different movements.
✧ Invite a child to mime the movements of a pet for the rest of the group to identify.

# PET FRIEND

* * * * * * * * * * * * * * * * * * * * * * * * * *

## Objective

RE – To examine the relationship between a child and a pet.

## Group size

Small groups (up to six children).

## What you need

A form for each child (a model version of this is given in Figure 1), pencils, crayons.

Pet friend.
I would choose a _ _ _ _ _ _ _

what I would do for my pet:

what my pet would do for me:

*Figure 1*

## What to do

Give each child a form and help them to read it through. Invite them to choose a pet, draw a picture of it in the box and complete the first sentence. An adult can act as scribe for younger children.

Discuss what each child would do for their pet, and help them to record their ideas on the form. Then discuss what the pet would do for the child, and write their suggestions on the form. Compare and contrast the children's choices of pets and their ideas about their relationship with a pet.

## Discussion

Encourage the children to consider the practical aspects of caring for a pet, such as feeding, watering, grooming and exercising. Talk about the need to give a pet love and affection as well as keeping it healthy and safe.

Move on to discussing the contribution a pet can make to the child's life. Talk about how a pet can return affection as well as being a friend and playmate.

## Follow-up activities

✧ Carry out a survey to find out what pets the children own.
✧ Discuss the painting 'Saint Francis and the Birds' by Sir Stanley Spencer (Tate Gallery) and use it to introduce the story of Saint Francis.
✧ Devise a list of rules for caring for a particular pet. Talk about what you would need to do every day (feeding, stroking) and what you would need to do every week (cleaning out cages, grooming).
✧ Read the poem 'But Me?' on page 67 of the Resources section.

# PET SOUNDS

## Objective

Music – To use a simple song to investigate animal sounds.

## Group size

Any size.

## What you need

An area to sit in.

## What to do

Change the words of the song 'Old MacDonald had a farm' to 'Old MacDonald had a pet shop'. Invite a child to choose the pet for each verse and suggest the sound it would make. Make up as many different verses as possible.

## Discussion

Talk about the type of sound each pet would make. Consider whether it would be high/low, long/short, fast/slow, loud/quiet. Why would a pet make noises? Reasons might include to convey happiness, anger, fear or a warning, or to ask for food, a walk or attention.

Encourage the children to include more unusual pets such as parrots, fish, stick insects and snails. Can they invent sounds for pets which make no obvious noise, such as a lizard or a tortoise?

## Follow-up activities

✧ Make a picture frieze of the animals in the song and include appropriate sounds in speech bubbles.
✧ Listen to tape-recorded sounds of real pets and try to identify the type of animal.
✧ Sing 'Granny Davey's House' (see page 82 of the Resources section).
✧ Act out a short role-play about a pet shop owner who is unable to sleep because of all the different sounds the pets make in his shop. Talk about how the owner could solve the problem.
✧ Create a group story about a dog who will not stop barking. An adult could act as scribe to record the children's ideas.

# CHAPTER 7
# DISPLAYS

Displays are a good way of stimulating children's interest. They can bring together a collection of the children's work or move the topic on to another sub-theme. A display can be made more meaningful to the children either by involving them in setting up the display or by encouraging them to interact with it.

## WHERE'S SPOT?

Links with Chapter One: Dogs.

### What you need

The story *Where's Spot?* by E. Hill (Picture Puffin), a display table covered in yellow crêpe paper, a picture (or soft toy) dog to represent Spot, a collection of different objects for Spot to hide in (such as a dolls' house, a toy van, a plastic teapot, a helmet, a basket, a cardboard wardrobe, a box), a felt-tipped pen, white card for the labels.

### Preparation

Read the story to the children. Invite individuals to open the flaps on each page in the search for Spot, who is missing at dinner-time.

### What to do

Arrange the collection of objects on the display table. Hide the picture or soft toy 'Spot' inside, under or behind one of the objects. Add a card label saying 'Where's Spot?'

Show the children the display and explain that they need to find out where Spot is hiding. Ask individuals to choose one object and look to see if Spot is hiding there. When Spot has been found, suggest that the child who has found him hides him in a different place so that the game can continue.

Maintain interest in the display by hiding Spot in different places throughout the day. Also encourage the children to find other objects for Spot to hide in, and add these to the display.

### Discussion

Ask the children to guess where Spot might be before they search. Talk with the children as they look for him. Name each object and reinforce positional vocabulary such as *behind, inside, under.*

### Follow-up activities

✧ Make the search for Spot more complex by hiding other animals (small pictures or plastic animals) inside the objects which are empty.
✧ Use construction toys or junk modelling to make other objects for Spot to hide in.

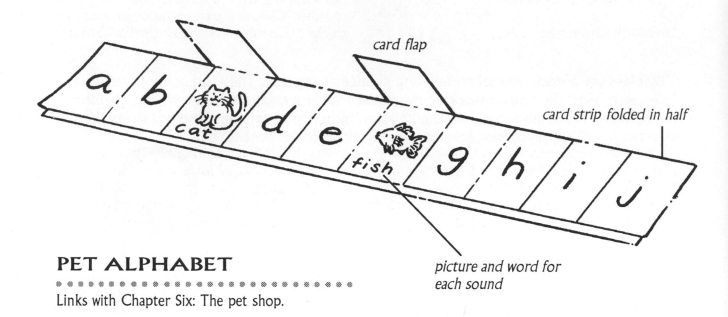

card flap

card strip folded in half

picture and word for each sound

## PET ALPHABET

Links with Chapter Six: The pet shop.

### What you need

Coloured card, a felt-tipped pen, small pieces of white paper, pencils, crayons, scissors, PVA adhesive, a display board, a stapler.

### What to do

Cut a long strip of card (you will probably need to join several sheets of card together) and fold it in half lengthways. Divide the top half into 26 sections of equal size, and cut slits so that there are 26 flaps. Label the outside face of each one with a letter of the alphabet. Draw or find a picture of a pet or pet care item for each letter, and label it (for example, a – aquarium, b – budgie, c – cat, and so on). Older children could be asked to suggest and draw their own pictures for most of the letters. As it is difficult to find pet examples for all the letters of the alphabet, draw some other animals or objects (e – elephant, z – zebra). Stick each picture on to the card strip underneath the corresponding flap (see illustration above).

Staple the alphabet frieze to a display board which the children can easily reach. Ask individuals to lift the flap for a specific letter to discover what's hidden underneath.

### Discussion

Talk about the picture shown under each flap. Is it a pet, or does it live in the zoo or on a farm?

Identify any pet care items and talk about their functions. Can the children suggest another example of a word which begins with the sound of the letter shown on the flap?

### Follow-up activities

✧ Find other animal alphabet books or friezes to look at.
✧ Make sound sheets. Cut out a large pet shape (such as a cat or budgie in a cage) and stick pictures of things beginning with the same sound as the pet on to the shape.

# FISH COLOURS

Links with Chapter Four: Fish.

## What you need

Two small tables, four paper fishing-net shapes (red, green, yellow, blue), a long piece of string, coloured wool (red, green, yellow, blue), newspaper, a stapler, sugar paper and different types of paper such as tissue, crêpe and foil (red, green, yellow, blue), PVA adhesive, spreaders, pencils, scissors. *NB* For children who are already very familiar with the colours suggested above, substitute less familiar ones such as brown, grey or purple.

## What to do

Invite the children to make some fish. Ask each child to choose a piece of coloured sugar paper, draw a fish on it and cut it out. They can draw round their fish shape on another sheet of sugar paper of the same colour and cut this out also. Decorate both the fish shapes by sticking different types of paper, in the same colour as the sugar paper, on to one side of each fish. As the fish shapes are going to be stapled together, make sure the children decorate the correct sides.

When the adhesive is dry, staple together the tail parts of the two fish halves. Place a small amount of screwed-up newspaper into the fish to pad it out slightly, and staple the edges of the fish together. Choose a piece of wool to match the colour of the fish, and staple one end on to the top of the fish.

Suspend a long piece of string above the two tables to make a line, and tie all the fish to it in colour groups. On the table below each colour group, place a matching paper fishing-net. (See illustration.)

Ask the children to find objects of the same colour as each set of fish and place them on the paper net below. Mix up the objects, or the fish, and ask the children to spot the mistakes and rearrange them correctly.

## Discussion

As the children make their fish, talk about the different-coloured papers they are using. Is their colour dark or pale, bright or dull? Similarly, discuss the colour of the objects that the children find for each set of fish.

## Follow-up activities

◇ Explore ways of making the fish mobiles move (this links with the 'Flapping fish' activity on page 40).

◇ Draw and shade a fish in one colour, using mixed media such as wax crayons, coloured pencils, chalks, pastels, oil pastels, collage materials.

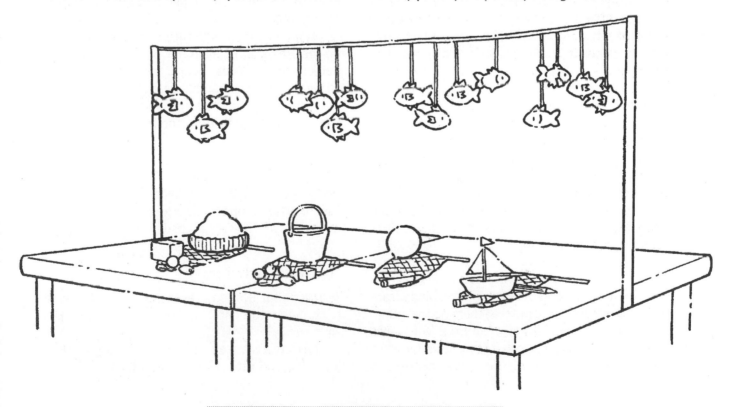

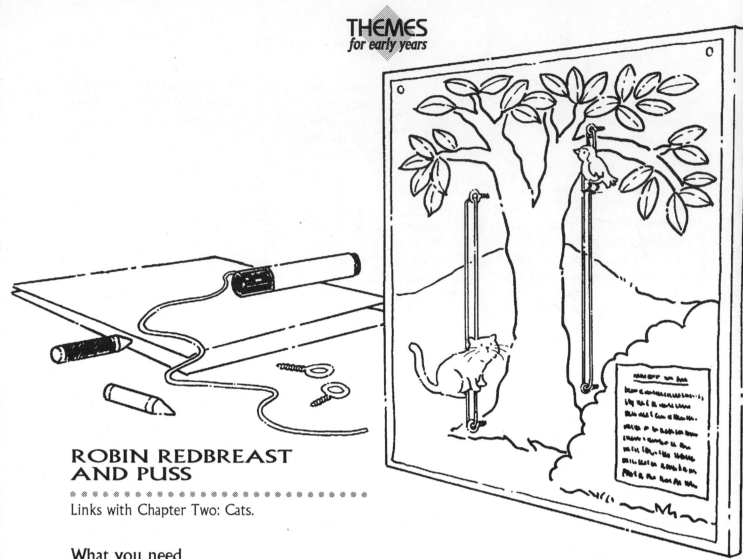

# ROBIN REDBREAST
# AND PUSS

Links with Chapter Two: Cats.

## What you need

A copy of the rhyme 'Robin Redbreast and Puss' on page 73 of the Resources section, a display board, blue and green backing paper, a stapler, scissors, brown sugar paper, wax crayons, green sugar paper, a black felt-tipped pen, white card, four small metal eye-hooks, string, adhesive tape.

## Preparation

Learn the rhyme.

## What to do

Cover the top half of the display board with blue backing paper. Cut a hill shape out of the green backing paper and use this to cover the bottom half of the display board.

Cut a large tree shape out of the brown sugar paper. Invite some children to add a bark texture by using the wax crayons to make rubbings from textured materials and putting them on the trunk.

Ask a group of children to cut out leaf shapes from the green sugar paper. They can add veins to the leaves with the wax crayons. Staple the tree and leaves to the display board.

Cut a bush shape from green sugar paper and write the rhyme on it. Staple the bush to one side of the tree.

Draw and colour a picture of a cat and a robin on the card and cut them out. Screw the four eye-hooks into the display board, thread two pieces of string through them and tie each string into a loop. Stick the cat on to one string and the robin on to the other using adhesive tape (see illustration).

## Discussion

Encourage the children to read the rhyme and to use the string loops to move the cat and the robin up and down the tree according to the rhyme.

## Follow-up activities

✧ Talk about how to prevent cats from catching birds. Show the children examples of cat collars with bells.
✧ Illustrate a simple food chain – caterpillar eats leaf, bird eats caterpillar, cat eats bird.

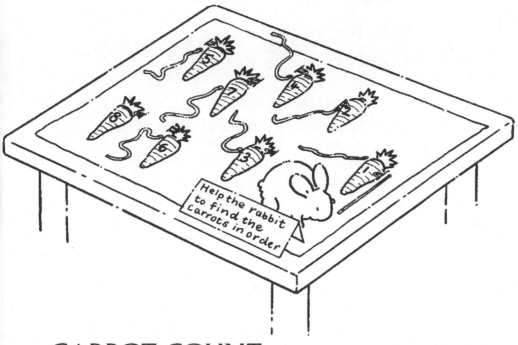

## CARROT COUNT

Links with Chapter Five: Rabbits.

### What you need

A small table with easy access all round, a large sheet of green card (approximately A1 size), small pieces of white card, felt-tipped pens, scissors, paper-clips, a Stanley knife, coloured laces, a soft toy rabbit.

### Preparation

On the white card, draw ten carrots of a sufficient size for a child to handle each one easily. Colour the carrots and label each one with a number from 1 to 10. Cut them out. If young children are not familiar with all the numbers to ten, adapt the activity to suit their abilities by reducing the number of carrots, for example to five.

### What to do

Tie a knot in the first lace, make a hole in the large sheet of card and thread the lace through. Measure how far the lace will reach along the card in any direction, and place carrot number 1 at the end of the lace. Hold the carrot in place by cutting a short slit in the green card with a Stanley knife and attaching the carrot in place with a paper-clip. Thread the second lace through the card adjacent to carrot number one and repeat as above. Continue adding laces and carrots until all the numbers are used up, finishing with the highest-numbered carrot. (See left illustration.)

Place the card sheet on the table and put the toy rabbit beside the first lace. Add a label saying 'Help the rabbit to find the carrots in order'.

### Discussion

Invite individual children to join the laces to the carrots to show the order in which the rabbit must eat the carrots (from 1 to 10). The child can do this by placing each lace so that it touches the next carrot with the correct number. If the children are familiar with dot-to-dot pictures, it may help if you compare the laces with the lines which they would draw.

Once the children are familiar with the activity, extend it by increasing the number of carrots (if you have only used five). Alternatively, move the carrots around to provide a different route.

### Follow-up activities

✧ Deliberately place the laces in the wrong order and ask a child to reorder them correctly.
✧ Devise simple dot-to-dot worksheets based on pictures associated with the rabbit theme, such as a carrot, a hutch or a rabbit.
✧ Make simple sewing cards using laces and pictures based on a rabbit theme.

# CHAPTER 8
# ASSEMBLIES

**Assemblies are the ideal way of bringing your children together to share their learning with others. The ideas in this chapter build on the experiences the children will have had in activities elsewhere in the book. They will encourage the children to think about their favourite pets and why they are special. All the ideas are also suitable for smaller group sharing times.**

## OUR FAVOURITE PETS

The focus for this approach is on the pets owned by children in the class or group.

The assembly involves the children in drawing on experiences they may already have had during other activities, such as painting or collage, sorting and matching tasks and observations of pets at home or elsewhere. These activities should have heightened their awareness of the wide variety of different animals kept as pets and the particular characteristics of each type.

The assembly will work in a range of settings, including a large gathering or a smaller group.

### Introduction

The person leading the assembly should begin by asking the children to focus on the work they have already done on pets — perhaps asking some of them to show their prints of dogs, wear their cat masks or demonstrate their pet movements.

### Activity

Children dressed to represent the different types of pets owned by members of the group should be invited to come forward, and those in the audience called upon to identify each animal. (Obviously this will require preparation work based on earlier sessions.)

For a small group, children could be asked to go and sit beside their favourite kind of pet. In a larger gathering, it might be more appropriate to ask for a show of hands in order to establish which animal is the most popular choice of pet.

This activity should help children to understand that there are many different types of animals kept as pets.

### Reflection

The assembly leader should encourage all the children to think about the pets they have seen represented during the assembly, and perhaps to think particularly of the one which they might choose as their favourite pet. The leader can remind the children that although they may have a particular favourite, others may choose a completely different type of pet (or perhaps none at all).

While the audience reflect on this for a few moments, the children representing the different animals can simulate their movements — showing how pets vary not only in appearance, but in many other ways too. This will be enhanced by appropriate background music — Saint-Saëns' *Carnival of the Animals* may contain some relevant pieces — or the children could attempt to recreate various animal noises, such as the purring of a kitten or the twittering of a bird.

## Prayer

Some children may welcome the opportunity to praise and thank God for creating so many different animals for them to appreciate, or may want to express gratitude for their own particular pets. They may like to compose their own prayers for the occasion, or the leader might choose one from an anthology.

## Song

Most groups will be familiar with a wide range of songs and rhymes which feature animals and pets; any of these would probably be suitable to close this gathering. The well-known hymn 'All things bright and beautiful' is also appropriate for those who prefer a piece which is specifically religious in character.

## AMAZING PETS

The focus for this approach is an exploration of which animals make suitable pets. The children will be encouraged to build on their awareness of the various characteristics of a wide range of animals and to evaluate which are appropriate in a pet.

## Introduction

The person leading the assembly should invite the children to think about as many different kinds of animals as possible; if necessary, various stimuli — such as pictures, slides, models, and so on — could be used.

In a small-group setting, it will be possible to invite a spontaneous response from the children; but with a larger gathering, it will be more appropriate to have prepared this with the children in advance. Their suggestions could be given verbally or in another form, such as a mime or role-play, or through pictures, drawings and models.

## Activity

The purpose of this activity is to give the children an insight into the practicalities of keeping an animal as a pet.

The leader reads out or tells the story *Dear Zoo* by Rod Campbell (Picture Puffin), in which the author tries to obtain a suitable pet from among the animals available in the zoo. In a small group, the children will enjoy lifting the flaps in the book to reveal which creature is concealed in each package. In larger gatherings, it might be more appropriate to involve the children in acting out the text, using costumes, masks and other props.

## Reflection

The leader should encourage the children to think about why each of the animals in the story — except for the dog — would not be suitable as a pet. They should be invited to consider all the advantages of having a dog as a companion and should also be reminded of a dog owner's various responsibilities.

## Prayer

Some children may like to have an opportunity to thank God for all the different animals in the world, especially pet dogs. It may be appropriate to use a prayer which also asks God to help dog owners to take proper care of their pets, ensuring that their dogs have sufficient food, water, exercise and affection. This could be composed by the person leading the assembly and, if possible, should include ideas contributed by some of the children.

## Song

The predictable choice here is 'How much is that doggy in the window?', but you may also wish to put some appropriate new words to a well-known tune — for example, 'Here we go round the mulberry bush' could become 'This is the way we walk our dog', and so on.

## PETS ARE SPECIAL

The focus for this approach is on the loving relationship which often exists between a child and a pet, and the feelings that may be experienced by a child when a pet dies.

While it is natural to hope that a young child will not have to confront the death of a loved person for many years, that is sadly not always the case. This assembly may offer support to children who have suffered bereavement, and also deals with the more common occurrence of the death of a well-loved pet.

### Introduction

The assembly leader should begin by asking the children to think of ways in which a person can show love and care for a pet dog. The children should be invited to think of practical considerations — a dog needs adequate exercise, proper grooming, a comfortable place to sleep — and should also be encouraged to recognise that a pet dog is also entitled to affection and love.

### Activity

The purpose of this activity is to give children an opportunity to reflect on the themes and concepts featured in the book *I'll Always Love You* by Hans Wilhelm (Knight, Hodder & Stoughton).

The story tells of the close and loving relationship between a young boy and his pet dog. The two of them share many happy times together, but as the boy grows bigger and stronger, the dog becomes ill and infirm and eventually dies. The boy is consoled with the knowledge that he not only cared for the dog, but also told her that he loved her. Although he is offered a new puppy by a neighbour, he declines the offer, realising that he cannot replace his pet and needs time in which to mourn her loss.

The story is simply told and well-illustrated. It is best presented in a small group, where the children feel secure and have the opportunity to discuss the text and respond to it through comments and questions.

### Reflection

The leader should encourage the children to think about the key elements of the story, emphasising the importance of expressing love and affection for pets and celebrating the companionship they offer.

### Prayer

Children may like to be given an opportunity to thank God for the happiness that pet animals have given to them; and if appropriate, to remember those they have loved who have died.

### Song

A soft, quiet melody without any words may be more appropriate here than a song. After a gathering such as this, where sensitive issues have been raised, it will be important not to break off suddenly from the mood or atmosphere which has been created.

*NB* Remember that not all the children will have pets at home, and this should be acknowledged during these sessions.

### Collective Worship in Schools

The assemblies outlined here are suitable for use with children in nurseries and playgroups, but would need to be adapted for use with pupils registered in schools. As a result of legislation enacted in 1944, 1988 and 1993, there are now specific points to be observed when developing a programme of Collective Acts of Worship in a school.

Further guidance will be available from your local SACRE — Standing Advisory Council for RE.

# ACTION RHYMES AND POEMS

## CATS

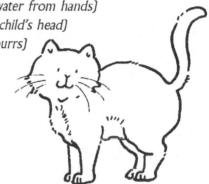

| | |
|---|---|
| Cats have furry tummies | (Circular strokes over tummy) |
| Cats have furry paws | (Stroke backs of hands) |
| Cats have swishy tails | (Pretend to swish tail) |
| And little sharp claws | (Curl fingers into claws) |
| | |
| They like to walk on tip-toe | (Walk on tip-toe) |
| They like to pounce and play | (Pounce and play with a paper ball) |
| They like to curl up small | (Curl up small) |
| And sleep all day | (Pretend to sleep) |
| | |
| Cats MIAOW when they're hungry | (Miaow and wave paws) |
| They MIAOW with wet fur | (Shake water from hands) |
| But if you stroke them gently | (Stroke child's head) |
| All they want to do is purr | (Child purrs) |

Jan Jones

## BUT ME?

Robert cleans his rabbit,
Chloe strokes her cat,
Hadjid holds his hamster,
Bethan likes her bat,
Tricia feeds her terrapin,
But me?
I hug my *rat!*

Barry loves his budgie,
Donna walks her dog,
Pasha trains his parrot,
Hi-Ching grooms her hog,
Derek rides his dapple-grey,
But me?
I kiss my *frog!*

Wes Magee

**PHOTOCOPIABLE RESOURCES**

# WHO TOOK THE CHEESE?
# (A CHANTING RHYME)

Who took the cheese?
*Squeak, squeak, squeak.*

Who took the bone?
*Bow-wow.*

Who took the carrot?
*Thump, thump, thump.*

Who took the milk?
*Miaow.*

Who took the apple?
*Crunch, crunch, crunch.*

Who took the corn seed?
*Cluck.*

Who took the lettuce leaf?
*Munch, munch, munch.*

Who took the lollipop?
*Suck.*

Tony Mitton

> **Note:** *This is a poem that can be treated in a variety of ways, but an obvious approach for younger children might be for the teacher to read or call out the questions and for the children to chorus the animal noises.*
>
> *Part of the fun can be for the children to guess the culprits from the noises; while most of these are obvious, one or two could prompt lively discussion.*
>
> *Alternatively, share the poem between groups of children, or give single noises to confident individuals to recite.*

## PHOTOCOPIABLE RESOURCES

# BLACK CAT

Black cat, what are you at?
Where are you going and why?
Why are your whiskers twitching like that?
Why does the fur lie flat on your back?
Why are you waving your tail in the air?
Why are your eyes open wide in a stare?
What are you watching there by the tree?
Is it a bird or a leaf you can see?
Black cat, just what are you at?

Jan Pollard

# GUINEA-PIGS

Two little guinea-pigs
black and white and friendly,
lived in our garden shed
and had a little family.
Four little guinea-pigs
grew and grew and grew
and soon they were just as big
as the very first two.
Six little guinea-pigs
some black, some white, some brown,
had eight little babies
so we took them all to town.
We took them to the pet shop
and hoped they'd buy them, when
on taking them out of the cardboard box
we found that there were TEN!

*(Count in twos, using your fingers; two, four, six,
eight, ten, with palms together.)*

Jan Pollard

# PET RIDDLES

I like carrots
to bite and crunch.
I like lettuce
for my lunch.
I like digging
(it's a habit).
I like thumping.
I'm a ...        (rabbit)

I'll lie in your lap
as you stroke my fur.
And if I feel drowsy
I'll doze and purr.
But if I should sniff
a mouse or a rat,
I'm off round the house
Can you guess?
I'm a ...        (cat)

# MY DOG'S FIRST POEM

*(To be read aloud in a dog-like voice.)*

My barking drives them
up the wall.
I chew the carpet
in the hall.
I love to chase
a bouncing, er, b....    (banana?)

Everywhere I leave
long hairs.
I fight the cushions
on the chairs.
Just watch me race
right up the, er, s....    (shower?)

Once I chewed
a stick of chalk.
I get bored when
the family talk.
Then someone takes me
for a, er, w....    (wheelbarrow?)

Wes Magee

I'll fetch you a stick
if you throw it and call.
I'll beg for a bone
and I'll bring back a ball.
I'm fond of a walk
or a run or a jog.
Surely you've guessed me now?
Yes, I'm a ...    (dog)

Tony Mitton

## PET FINGERS

Dogs run
— let your fingers run.
Frogs leap
— let your fingers leap.
Fish swim
— let your fingers swim.
And cats creep
— let your fingers creep.

Rabbits hop
— let your fingers hop.
Parrots talk
— let your fingers talk.
Snakes glide
— let your fingers glide.
And ponies walk
— let your fingers walk.

*(Actions — as indicated in the verses.)*

Wes Magee

## BARNEY AND FRED

Fancy eating your bed
Like the guinea-pigs Barney and Fred
Who nibble away
Wood shavings and hay.

I should never feel
Like making my house a meal
And gnawing the wood
To do my teeth good.

I never met anyone yet
Who ate the floor and carpet
Except, as I said,
Barney and Fred.

Stanley Cook

# NEXT DOOR'S DINOSAUR

Do your neighbours have a puppy?
Do they own a family cat?
The folk who live next door to us
keep a Dinosaur called Drat!

It must have been a year ago
they heard thumping at the door,
and when they went to answer it
they were shocked by what they saw.

Standing squarely in the garden,
her neck reaching to the roof,
was Drat the dreaded Dinosaur
in a yellow waterproof!

Drat quickly made herself at home
(for breakfast preferred kippers);
She commandeered a dressing-gown
and a pair of pure wool slippers.

She tried sleeping on the sofa,
she tried sleeping in the bed;
but every time she tossed and turned
she bumped her bulky head.

So her tail fits in the bedroom,
her back legs fill the bath.
Her neck twists around the living room
and up the garden path!

John Rice

# PET TALK

## JUMPING HERE, JUMPING THERE

Jumping here, jumping there
Jumping, jumping everywhere!
I can bounce and I can hop!
See me run, and see me stop!
One last jump to finish, so
Leap up high and jump down low.

Kate Harrison

Jamie has a cat,
Jimmy has a dog;
Jennie has a gerbil,
Jilly has a frog.

Mandy has a budgie,
Michael has a horse;
Maggie has a rabbit
and I have...
a BABY BROTHER,
of course!

Judith Nicholls

## ROBIN REDBREAST AND PUSS

Little Robin Redbreast sat upon a tree
Up went Pussycat and down went he.
Down came Pussycat and away Robin ran,
Says little Robin Redbreast, 'Catch me if you can'.

Little Robin Redbreast flew up on the wall,
Pussycat jumped after him and almost had a fall.
Little Robin chirped and sang, and what did Pussy say?
Pussycat said, 'Mew,' and Robin flew away.

Barbara Ireson

# DRAT THAT FAT CAT!
## (A JOINING–IN STORY)

Once there was a cat, a fat, fat cat. But was that cat fat enough?

NO, HE WAS NOT.

So he padded along the path in search of food.

The fat cat met a rat.

'Have you any food, rat?'

'No, I have not,' said the rat.

'Too bad, then. I must eat *you* up.'

'But you are fat enough already!'

But was that fat cat fat enough?

NO, HE WAS NOT.

So he gobbled up the rat and padded along the path in search of food, with the rat going 'Squeak, squeak, squeak,' inside him.

The fat cat met a duck.

'Have you any food, duck?'

'No, I have not,' said the duck.

'Too bad, then. I must eat *you* up.'

'But you are fat enough already!'

But was that cat fat enough?

NO, HE WAS NOT.

So he gobbled up the duck and padded down the path in search of food, with the duck going 'Quack, quack, quack,' and the rat going 'Squeak, squeak, squeak,' inside him.

The fat cat met a dog.

'Have you any food, dog?'

'No, I have not,' said the dog.

'Too bad, then. I must eat *you* up.'

'But you are fat enough already!'

But was that cat fat enough?

NO, HE WAS NOT.

So he gobbled up the dog and padded along the path in search of food with the dog going 'Woof, woof, woof,' the duck going 'Quack, quack, quack,' and the rat going 'Squeak, squeak, squeak,' inside him.

The fat cat met an old lady.

'Have you any food, old lady?'

'No, I have not,' said the old lady.

'Too bad, then. I must eat *you* up.'

PHOTOCOPIABLE RESOURCES

'But you are fat enough already!'
But was that fat cat fat enough?
NO, HE WAS NOT.
So he gobbled up the old lady and padded along the path in search of food, with the old lady going 'Drat that fat cat,' the dog going 'Woof, woof, woof,' the duck going 'Quack, quack, quack,' and the rat going 'Squeak, squeak, squeak,' inside him.

A bee buzzed round the fat cat's head and, without a thought, he swallowed it whole.

The bee buzzed around inside the fat cat, where he found a rat going 'Squeak, squeak, squeak,' a duck going 'Quack, quack, quack,' a dog going 'Woof, woof, woof,' and an old lady going 'Drat that fat cat,' inside him.

'This is an outrage!' buzzed the bee. 'There isn't any room to swing a cat in here.'

The fat cat had forgotten that bees sting.
'Ow!' cried the fat cat. 'Meeow, ow, ow!' And he got the hiccups.

'Hic,' went the cat and out popped the bee.

'Hic,' went the cat and out popped the rat.

'Hic,' went the cat and out popped the duck.

'Hic,' went the cat and out popped the dog.

'Hic,' went the cat and out popped the old lady.

'Dear me,' said the old lady, 'what a very thin cat. Come home with me and I'll fatten you up.' The cat padded along the path behind her, in search of food, going 'Hic, hic, hic,' all the way home.

So was that cat now fat enough?
NO, HE WAS NOT!

Pat Thomson

# THE WAY OUT

Thompson was a long-haired hamster. He was very clean and very curious. He belonged to a boy called Luke.

Thompson's cage was in Luke's bedroom. It was a good-sized cage, with an upstairs and a downstairs. It had a newspaper nest inside a sleeping compartment, drinking water in a bottle on the side, a wheel and two ladders.

Thompson slept all day, but when night-time came he was up and about. He ran around his cage, up and down his ladders, round and round in his wheel. But that wasn't enough.

Thompson wanted to find the way out.

One night, after Luke had gone to bed, Thompson saw that his cage door was open! Thompson stayed still for a minute, sat on his hind legs, smartened up his whiskers and listened. He could feel the big room all around him!

He scrambled through the open door and toppled on to the bedroom floor. Across the carpet he scuttled, under the bed, into the cupboard, along the shelves, in and out of shoes, in between Luke's toys. But that still wasn't enough.

Thompson wanted to find the way out.

So he gnawed at the skirting board and scraped his way through. Thompson stayed still for a moment, pricked up his ears and listened. He could feel the big house all around him!

Through the bedroom he ran, in and out of the bathroom, before scrambling all the way downstairs. He went into the living-room, behind the sofa, in and out of drawers, under the door and into the kitchen. Even so, that wasn't enough.

Thompson wanted to find the way out.

Then he smelt something through the cat-flap in the door. Fresh air! He flipped through on to the path outside. There he stayed still for a moment, took a deep breath and listened. He could feel the big town all around him!

Across the garden he ran, through the gate, all along the street, past the shops and schools, until he reached the middle of the town. Even so, that wasn't enough.

Thompson wanted to find the way out.

Then he saw a bus waiting at the bus-stop. Thompson stayed still for a moment, cocked his head on one side and listened. He could sense the big country all around him!

So he stowed away on the bus and went through villages, towns and cities. He hopped on and off trains which took him up hill and down dale. He ran through forests and over fields until he came to the edge of the land. Yet still that wasn't enough.

Thomspon wanted to find the way out.

Then he saw the wide open sea. Thompson sat still for a moment, polished his nose with his paws and listened. He could feel the real world all around him!

So he stowed away on a ship, to the North Pole and the South Pole. And he stowed away on aeroplanes to the East and to the West. Soon he had been right round the world! But it just wasn't enough.

Thompson wanted to find the way out.

He looked up at the great empty sky. Thompson sat still for a moment, heaved a big sigh and listened. He could feel outer space all above him!

So he stowed away on a rocket to the moon. He ran all around the moon, in and out of craters. Then he jumped on to a shooting star which took him to the edge of the universe.

He peeped over the edge of the universe. He saw an endless big black hole!

E-E-E-K!

Thompson had had quite enough. He wanted to find the way home.

Thompson sat still for a moment, stood on his hind legs and suddenly felt very dizzy. He covered his eyes with his paws and fell into the big black hole.

Down and down he went, very fast and far, until he landed with a very soft bump.

Thompson uncovered his eyes. He was back inside Luke's room.

'Where have you been?' cried Luke. 'I've been looking everywhere for you!' Luke picked him up and stroked him and put him back inside his cage, with an upstairs and a downstairs for a wheel and two ladders.

Thompson sat still for a moment, then he had some biscuit for breakfast and a drink from his bottle. He smoothed down his fur and curled up in his newspaper nest.

How cosy and sleepy he felt! How very safe and sound!

Joyce Dunbar

*PHOTOCOPIABLE RESOURCES*

# MORAG AND THE LAMB

'Now be good — both of you!' said Mother. She drove off, leaving Russell and Morag to stay with Grandma and Grandpa.

'Why does everyone tell us to be good?' asked Russell. 'We *are* good.'

Morag barked to show that she agreed.

Grandma said, 'It's lambing time.'

Grandpa said, 'Russell, you must see that Morag doesn't worry the sheep.'

Russell said, 'Morag, you *mustn't* worry the sheep.'

The farmer came along the road in her canary-red tractor. 'I'm going to feed the sheep,' she said. 'Would you like to come along, Russell?'

'Oh yes, please!' said Russell.

Morag waved her tail. 'We'd better not take Morag,' said the farmer, 'just in case she tries to worry the sheep.'

Russell was puzzled. Why should she worry the sheep?

'It's a serious matter when dogs worry sheep,' said the farmer. 'If they do they often have to be put away.'

Put away?

Russell turned pale.

So did Morag, under her fur.

Russell said, 'Morag, you really must not worry the sheep.'

Grandpa lifted Russell up.

'Hold tight, now!' said Grandma.

Morag was left behind. She went slowly down the garden, keeping close to the dry-stone wall.

She pricked up her ears. What was that?

'*Baa-aa. Baa-aa.*'

She jumped over the wall into the next field. Then she saw the lamb.

The lamb was all tangled up in a bramble bush.

Morag pushed her head into the jaggy bush until their noses were almost touching. The lamb smelt strange.

She wriggled closer and their noses went bump!

'Baa-aa-aaa,' cried the lamb. It looked very worried.

But Morag hadn't worried it, had she?
What would happen if the farmer thought she had? Would she be put away?

She leapt over a stream and galloped up the field. The wind rushed in her ears. Then she saw Russell.

She barked loudly, once... twice... three times, telling him to come and follow her.

'Oh, Morag!' said Russell.

Morag looked up at him with anxious eyes. *Had* she worried the lamb?

'We must get help,' said Russell.

'Baa-aa,' cried the lamb.

'Come quickly!' Russell yelled.

The farmer began to run down the field towards them.

'Goodness me!' said the farmer. 'You are in a tangle.'

She eased aside the branches of the bramble bush and set the lamb free.

'Good boy, Russell!' said the farmer.

'It was Morag who found the lamb,' said Russell.

'*Very* good girl, Morag,' said the farmer.

'Morag didn't worry the lamb, did she?' asked Russell.

'Of course not!' said the farmer. 'To worry sheep means to chase and try to hurt them.'

'Morag would never, ever do that,' said Russell and Morag barked, once... twice... three times, to show that she agreed.

Joan Lingard

# KATY'S PETS

Katy wanted a pet, but Mum and Dad didn't. They said they'd got their hands full with baby Sam.

'Couldn't I have a little puppy?' asked Katy. 'I promise I'll look after it. Please?'

Mum shook her head firmly. 'Dogs bark all the time and have to be taken for long walks. And they get muddy paws everywhere.'

'What about a kitten, then?' asked Katy. 'You don't have to take cats for a walk and they're very clean. They're always washing themselves.'

'And they sharpen their claws on the furniture,' said Dad. 'We're not having a kitten.'

Katy thought hard. There must be some pet that Mum and Dad would approve of.

'How about a hamster?' she suggested. 'I could keep it in a cage in my bedroom. It won't be any trouble at all.'

Mum and Dad didn't like that idea either.

'Animals in cages have to be cleaned out regularly, Katy,' said Mum.

Dad agreed. 'Pets might be nice to play with, but all animals have to be looked after,' he said.

'That's why I want a pet, so I can look after it,' Katy told him.

Dad looked thoughtful. Then he looked out of the window and smiled. 'So you want something to look after, eh? Well, I think I've got the very thing.'

He went out to the garden and into the shed. Not long after, he called Katy outside. And there, right in the middle of

the garden, was a funny sort of table on a long stick of wood.

'What's that?' asked Katy.

'It's a bird table,' said Dad. 'Birds can't find food for themselves in the winter, so many of them die. You can look after them by putting some food on this table.'

Katy thought that was a brilliant idea.

Mum gave her some brown breadcrumbs and scraps of potatoes and cheese. 'The birds will like this,' she said.

Then Katy and Dad cut the food up into little bits and put it on the bird table, with a big bowl of water.

'We'd better go inside now,' said Dad. 'The birds won't eat while we're here.'

They all watched through the window. After a couple of minutes, two birds flew down on to the table and started eating. Then a few more. Katy laughed as two birds squabbled over a piece of bacon. Dad told Katy some of the birds' names; there was a chaffinch and a sparrow and a thrush.

When all the food had gone, the birds all flew away.

'Will they come back again?' asked Katy.

'They'll come back every day if you leave food out for them,' Dad told her. 'Do you think you can remember to do that?'

Katy nodded excitedly. 'I'll feed them every day,' she promised. 'I don't need a pet now. I can look after the birds instead.'

Mum and Dad were pleased about that. So were the birds.

Karen King

# SONGS

## PETS

2. I've got a goldfish.
I've got a spider.
I've got a dog that I can
Take for walks.

3. I've got a gerbil.
I've got a tortoise.
I've got a parrot
Though he never talks.

Clive Barnwell

# GRANNY DAVEY'S HOUSE

Chorus

Gran - ny Dav - ey had a house, Ee - i - add - ee - o. Gran - ny Dav - ey

had a house, Add - ee - o - the day. Gran - ny Dav - ey had a house,

All her pets lived in that house, What a rack - et filled that house, Ee - i - add - ee -

o! 1: Woof woof the dog would go, Woof woof the dog would go,

Woof woof the dog would go, But the gold - fish just went glug!

2. Meow meow the cat would go,
the cat would go,
the cat would go,
But the goldfish just went glug.

3. Squeak squeak the mouse would go, etc.
4. Tweet tweet the budgie said, etc.
5. Oink oink the pig would go, etc.
And so on ....

## Variations

*Sing as a cumulative song by singing verse 2 and adding verse 1 before the chorus, then verse 3 with verses 2 and 1, and so on.*

*Split the class into several groups, each group taking just one pet, and then for the final verse have all the groups singing their verses in one great cacophony.*

Ian R. Henderson-Begg

# MY DOG SANDY

**D**                                 **Em**

1. My dog *San - dy loves to run, run, run, When I

**A7**                        **D**                             **D7**

take him in the Park we go with Mum, Mum, Mum. Does - n't mat - ter if it's rain or

**G**      **Gm**              **D**            **A7**             **D**

sun, sun, sun. 'Cos for San - dy, Mum and me it's so much fun, fun, fun!

\* Children can substitute their own choice of name.

2. My dog Sandy loves to eat, eat, eat,
When I fill his bowl with food his tail will beat, beat, beat.
Crunchy biscuits all mixed up with meat, meat, meat,
Then a chocolate drop for pudding is a treat, treat, treat!
3. My dog Sandy loves to bark, bark, bark,
When the post arrives he pounces like a shark, shark, shark.
Spooky noises scare him when it's dark, dark, dark.
And then Sandy sings as sweetly as a lark, lark, lark!

*A possible variation is for the leader to sing the first part of each line,
and the children to sing (or shout) the three words at the end
of each line. Children could also substitute their own choice of name.*

Peter Morrell

# COME TO THE PET SHOP

Come to the pet shop, come with me. Let's go and see what we can see.

There's a lit - tle pup - py all a - lone. He needs a nice kind home.

Collect some pictures of baby animals the children might see in a pet shop.
(You could use toys instead of pictures.)
Set these out at the front of the class.
Each time you sing a verse, invite one of the children to choose an animal.
This song gives you an opportunity to discuss with the children what a baby
animal would need in a new home.

Jan Holdstock

# THE RABBIT'S WARNING

1. Thump, thump, there's dan - ger a - bout, that's the rab - bit's warn - ing

sound. Thump, thump, they're leav - ing their play. Thump, thump, they're

run - ning a - way till they're safe - ly un - der - ground.

Discuss with the children what kinds of things would frighten
the rabbits, and use these to replace the word 'danger'.
For example: for Verse 2, 'there's dogs about'.
For Verse 3, 'there's men about'.
For Verse 4, 'there's foxes about'.

Jan Holdstock

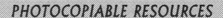

# WHO AM I?

1. Round and round, and round and round, Swim - ming all____ day long. Blow - ing bub - bles, swish - ing fins, Ne - ver make____ a sound.____

2. Fetch the stick, go fetch the stick,
Dashing to and fro.
Panting, barking, wagging tail,
Give a friendly lick.
3. Stroke my fur, please stroke my fur,
Sleeping in the sun.
Yawning, stretching, arching back,
Listen to me purr.

Gillian Parker

PHOTOCOPIABLE RESOURCES

# I'M A DOG WITH A JOB

1. I'm a dog with a job. Bow wow wow, I'm a dog with a job. Bow wow wow, I'm going to herd these sheep for you, that's a ve-ry good job for a dog to do and that's my job, Bow wow wow.

> 2. I'm going to see the way for you.
> 3. I'm going to catch those crooks for you.
> 4. I'm going to win this race for you.

*Try replacing 'Bow wow wow' with three claps, or with three sounds on an instrument.*

Jan Holdstock

# NAUGHTY LITTLE KITTEN

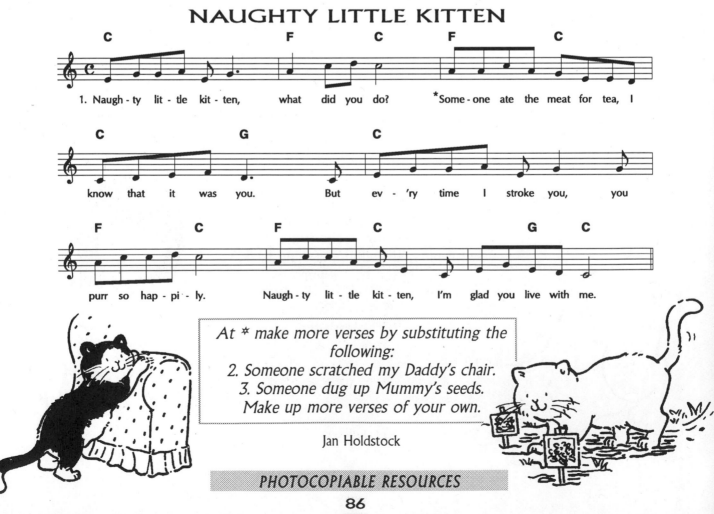

1. Naugh-ty lit-tle kit-ten, what did you do? *Some-one ate the meat for tea, I know that it was you. But ev-'ry time I stroke you, you purr so hap-pi-ly. Naugh-ty lit-tle kit-ten, I'm glad you live with me.

> *At \* make more verses by substituting the following:*
> *2. Someone scratched my Daddy's chair.*
> *3. Someone dug up Mummy's seeds.*
> *Make up more verses of your own.*

Jan Holdstock

**PHOTOCOPIABLE RESOURCES**

# PETS NEED LOOKING AFTER

1. Pets need a home like you and me. Pets need look-ing af - ter.

They need a bed, they need to be fed. They love to play with you ev - 'ry day.

You'll have a friend you can trust and love, But pets need look-ing af - ter.

> 2. Pets need a home like you and me.
> Pets need looking after.
> They like to be
> With a family.
> They will be fun
> And good company.
> You'll have a friend you can trust and love,
> But pets need looking after.

Jan Gilbert

**PHOTOCOPIABLE RESOURCES**

THEMES
*for early years*

Name _____

# Me and my dog

Match one dog to each child.

Draw a ball for each dog.

**THEMES**
*for early years*

Name _____

# Purring pairs

Draw the missing parts to make each pair of cats the same.

**THEMES**
*for early years*

# Living in fur

Join the dotted lines to get each guinea-pig home.

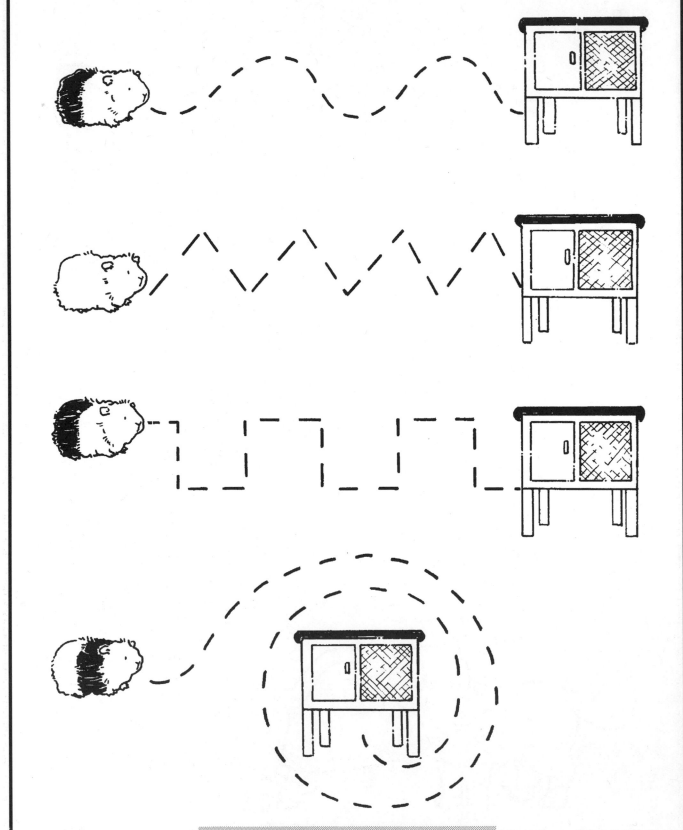

**THEMES**
*for early years*

Name _____

# Fish scales

Colour in to make patterns.

**THEMES**
*for early years*

# Fish numbers

Name _____

**THEMES** *for early years*

Name _____

# The rabbit's letters

Colour in the pictures which begin with the same sound as rabbit.

Now practise writing the letter **r** as shown below.

**THEMES**
*for early years*

# Rabbit numbers

Colour and count.
Colour the legs. How many legs?

Colour the ears. How many ears?

Colour the tails. How many tails?

**THEMES**
*for early years*

Name _____

# Which shop?

Match each item to the correct shop.

Pet shop

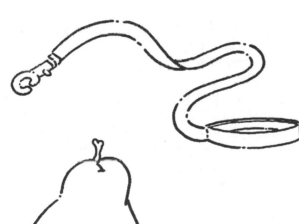

Greengrocer's

Toy shop

# RECOMMENDED MATERIALS

## INFORMATION BOOKS

*Looking After Your Dog* H. Piers (Frances Lincoln).
*Find a Pet* J. Tuinman (Schofield and Sims).
*Small Pets* R. Hill (Usborne).
*Dogs and Puppies* R. Hill (Usborne).
*The Puppy Book* C. Jessel (Walker).
*The Kitten Book* C. Jessel (Walker).
*I Love Guinea-Pigs* D. King-Smith (Walker).
*Rabbits* J. Williams (Picture Puffin).
*Pets* M. Daniels (Blackie).
*Althea's Pet* series R. Creek (Dinosaur Publications).
*Pets* Eye Openers Series (Dorling Kindersley).
*Taking Care of Your Pets* series (Franklin Watts).
*The Life Cycle of a Rabbit* J. Williams (Wayland).
*Hamster* B. Watts (A & C Black).

## STORY BOOKS

*Spot the Dog* series E. Hill (Picture Puffin).
*Our Puppy's Holiday* R. Brown (Andersen Press).
*Canonball Simp* J. Burningham (Dinosaur Publications).
*Harry the Dirty Dog* G. Zion (Bodley Head).
*Mog* series J. Kerr (Picture Lions).
*Meg and Mog* series H. Nicoll (Puffin).
*My Cat Likes to Hide in Boxes* E. Sutton (Puffin).
*Our Cat Flossie* R. Brown (Beaver Books).
*Tom's Cat* C. Voake (Walker Books).
*Mary's Pets* C. Scruton (Walker Books).
*Barnabus Walks* W. Mayne (Walker Books).
*Olga Da Polga* series M. Bond (Young Puffin).
*Guinea-Pigs Don't Read Books* C. Stanley Bare (Hippo).
*But No Elephants* J. Smath (Hippo).
*Fishes* B. Wildsmith (Oxford).
*Gertie's Goldfish* B. Gillham (Methuen).
*The Cat, the Fish and the Fish Tank* N. Lowenstein (Dinosaur Publications).
*Pet Show* E. Jack Keats (Puffin).
*Benjamin* series A. Baker (Picture Lions).
*Gerbil's Outing* and *Hamster is Hiding* H. Piers (Methuen).
*My Naughty Little Sister* and *Bad Harry's Rabbit* D. Edwards (Methuen).
*Schnitzel von Krumm's Basketwork* L. Dodd (Spindlewood).
'Living Things' section from *Stories to Read Aloud* (Scholastic).

## POETRY

'The Dog on the Beach', 'Goldfish' and 'Wanted' from *Rhyme Time 2* (Beaver Books).
'Sunning', 'Cat' and 'The Pet Shop' from *Young Puffin Book of Verse*.
*A Squirrel in Town* (Blackie).
*The Animal Fair* (Viking).
*Pet Poems* (Faber).
*Cat Poems* (OUP).
'Animals' section from *Early Years Poems and Rhymes* (Scholastic).
'The Diners in the Kitchen' J. Whitcomb Riley, *Rhymes of Childhood* from *A Golden Treasury of Animal Verse* – out of print (Pavilion).

## MUSIC

'Where Has My Little Doggie Gone', 'Daddy Wouldn't Buy Me a Bow Wow', 'Rabbit Ain't Got' and 'Risha, Rasha, Rusha' from *Apusskidu: 56 Songs For Children* (A & C Black).
'Bingo' and 'The Pet Shop Chorus' from *Sing a Song 2* (Nelson).
'A Little Fish' from *Sing a Song 1* (Nelson).
'Ding Dong Bell' from *Sing Hey Diddle Diddle* (A & C Black).
'3 Little Fishes' from *Topic Anthologies for Young Children – Water* (OUP).
'Pets' from *Sing As You Grow* (Ward Lock Educational).
'My Pets' from *Songs* (Scholastic).

## ART

'Two Cats' and 'Dog Before the World' Franz Marc.
'A Hound and a Bitch in a Landscape' George Stubbs.
'Portrait of Miss Bowles with her Dog' Reynolds.
'Pomeranian Bitch and Puppy' Thomas Gainsborough.
'Tama, the Japanese Dog' Pierre-Auguste Renoir.
'Grrr!' Roy Lichtenstein.
'Dog' Elizabeth Frink.

## INFORMATION SOURCES

*Animals and Plants in Schools: Legal Aspects* booklet Department for Education, Sanctuary Buildings, Great Smith Street, London SW1P 3BT.
*Animals in Schools* booklet RSPCA, Causeway, Horsham, West Sussex RH12 1HG.

*PHOTOCOPIABLE RESOURCES*